Mobile Devices

Practical Guides for Librarians

ⓖ About the Series

This innovative series written and edited for librarians by librarians provides authoritative, practical information and guidance on a wide spectrum of library processes and operations.

Books in the series are focused, describing practical and innovative solutions to a problem facing today's librarian and delivering step-by-step guidance for planning, creating, implementing, managing, and evaluating a wide range of services and programs.

The books are aimed at beginning and intermediate librarians needing basic instruction/guidance in a specific subject and at experienced librarians who need to gain knowledge in a new area or guidance in implementing a new program/service.

ⓖ About the Series Editor

The **Practical Guides for Librarians** series was conceived by and is edited by M. Sandra Wood, MLS, MBA, AHIP, FMLA, Librarian Emerita, Penn State University Libraries.

M. Sandra Wood was a librarian at the George T. Harrell Library, the Milton S. Hershey Medical Center, College of Medicine, Pennsylvania State University, Hershey, PA, for over thirty-five years, specializing in reference, educational, and database services. Ms. Wood worked for several years as a development editor for Neal-Schuman Publishers.

Ms. Wood received an MLS from Indiana University and an MBA from the University of Maryland. She is a fellow of the Medical Library Association and served as a member of MLA's Board of Directors from 1991 to 1995. Ms. Wood is founding and current editor of *Medical Reference Services Quarterly*, now in its thirty-fifth volume. She also was founding editor of the *Journal of Consumer Health on the Internet* and the *Journal of Electronic Resources in Medical Libraries* and served as editor/coeditor of both journals through 2011.

Titles in the Series

Mobile Devices
A Practical Guide for Librarians

Ben Rawlins

PRACTICAL GUIDES FOR LIBRARIANS, No. 12

ROWMAN & LITTLEFIELD
Lanham • Boulder • New York • London

Published by Rowman & Littlefield
A wholly owned subsidiary of The Rowman & Littlefield Publishing Group, Inc.
4501 Forbes Boulevard, Suite 200, Lanham, Maryland 20706
www.rowman.com

16 Carlisle Street, London W1D 3BT, United Kingdom

British Library Cataloguing in Publication Information Available

Library of Congress Cataloging-in-Publication Data
Rawlins, Ben, 1982–
    Mobile devices : a practical guide for librarians / Ben Rawlins.
        pages cm. — (Practical guides for librarians ; 12)
    Includes bibliographical references and index.
    ISBN 978-0-8108-9258-3 (pbk. : alk. paper) — ISBN 978-0-8108-9259-0 (ebook)
    1. Mobile communication systems—Library applications. 2. Public services (Libraries)—
Technological innovations. I. Title.
    Z680.5.R39 2015
    025.042—dc23   2014026972

♾™ The paper used in this publication meets the minimum requirements of American
National Standard for Information Sciences—Permanence of Paper for Printed Library
Materials, ANSI/NISO Z39.48-1992.

Printed in the United States of America

Contents

List of Illustrations

Figures

Table

List of Textboxes

Preface

The release of the iPhone in 2007 was a catalyst for the mainstream adoption of mobile technology. While it is true that mobile technology existed before the introduction of the iPhone, Apple's device gave us a glimpse into what was possible with mobile technology. Not only did we have a cell phone, we had a smartphone—a mobile device that was able to make calls, send text messages, check e-mails, browse the Web, and run applications. It was built on an operating system specifically designed for a mobile device. The success of the iPhone led many other technology companies to begin developing smartphones, and Google created the rival mobile operating system Android. Mobile devices have significantly changed the way that we, as a society, access information. They have also changed what we expect to be able to do with our devices. No longer are these devices just about accessing information; they have become entrenched in our lives. They are now starting to control our other electronic devices, and in some cases our home security systems.

The rapid adoption of mobile technology has had a significant impact on various facets of society, one of those being libraries. With more users coming to the library equipped with mobile devices, librarians need to develop the necessary skills to reach this growing user base. Developing and offering mobile services and resources can seem like a daunting and intimidating task, but rest assured it can be done, and done well. *Mobile Devices: A Practical Guide for Librarians* will give you a broad overview of the current mobile landscape, what it means for libraries, and how to determine what mobile devices to target, along with practical ideas and examples of how to use mobile devices in a variety of ways. Among other things, *Mobile Devices* includes snippets of code for mobile websites and native applications for the iOS and Android mobile operating systems to give you a starting point.

Additionally, *Mobile Devices: A Practical Guide for Librarians* will aid you and your library as you go through the process of planning, developing, implementing, marketing, and evaluating mobile services. Based on research and experience using and developing mobile websites and applications, this book includes information and ideas regarding:

- Why mobile technologies are important for libraries
- Developing mobile websites and applications for specific mobile platforms such as iOS and Android using existing Web technologies such as HTML, CSS, and JavaScript

- Marketing strategies to make users aware of mobile services
- Evaluating mobile services
- Emerging mobile technology

This book is aimed at librarians interested in mobile technologies, both beginners and experienced librarians, who are looking for ideas and examples of how to implement mobile technologies and services. *Mobile Devices: A Practical Guide for Librarians* contains eleven chapters. Chapter 1, "Why Mobile Matters," provides a broad overview of the current mobile landscape, as well as the adoption of various mobile devices like smartphones, tablets, and e-readers. It contains information regarding the expanding use of these devices and the potential that many corporations see in mobile technology.

The continued development in mobile technology has dramatically shifted what users expect from their mobile devices. Chapter 2, "User Expectations and the Impact of Mobile Technologies on Libraries," focuses on the changing nature of user expectations regarding mobile devices and the interactions that they expect. With the increased expectations of mobile users, library services and resources have been affected, as libraries look to provide users access to information in a mobile-optimized format.

Your library understands the importance of mobile technology and the impact that it is having on the information behavior of users. Now you need to decide and plan what types of mobile services and resources your library will offer. Chapter 3, "Deciding on and Planning Mobile Library Services and Resources," offers suggestions on what mobile devices and operating systems your library should target. There are also suggestions on what to consider when offering mobile services and resources to your users.

The next three chapters focus on developing mobile websites and applications for iOS and Android. Chapter 4, "Developing Mobile-Optimized Library Websites," focuses on the different mobile frameworks available to develop a mobile library website, as well as snippets of code from the jQuery Mobile framework. Responsive Web design is another option for developing a library website. Chapter 5, "Developing Library Applications for iOS," discusses the PhoneGap framework, which can be used to develop native applications for the iOS platform using existing Web technologies such as HTML, CSS, and JavaScript. It also walks you through the guidelines and requirements for submitting your library application to the App Store for approval and distribution. Chapter 6, "Developing Library Applications for Android," discusses how the PhoneGap framework can be used to develop native applications for the Android platform using existing Web technologies. It also walks you through the guidelines and requirements for submitting your library application to Google Play for distribution.

In addition to providing your users with library-developed mobile websites and applications, there are a variety of mobile-based resources offered by library vendors. Chapter 7, "Mobile Websites and Applications Offered by Library Vendors," covers these.

There are many different ways you can provide mobile services to your users, as well as library personnel, without developing mobile websites and applications. Chapter 8, "Mobile Services and Solutions for Users and Library Personnel," provides examples of different mobile services that libraries are using to reach mobile users. It also covers ways that mobile devices can be used by library personnel.

After you have launched your mobile services and resources, you will need to evaluate and update them. Chapter 9, "Evaluating and Maintaining Your Mobile Services and Resources," recommends ways you can evaluate and maintain the mobile services and resources of your library. It also covers how to submit an update for your library application to the App Store and Google Play.

Once you have developed mobile services and resources, you will want to ensure that your users are aware of them. Chapter 10, "Marketing Your Library's Mobile Services and Resources," offers suggestions on ways that you can let your users know about them.

With the rapid adoption of mobile technology, companies are looking to develop the next wave of emerging mobile devices. Chapter 11, "Emerging Mobile Technology," discusses emerging technologies and their potential applications in libraries. Examples of libraries that are exploring some of these new technologies are provided.

As mobile technology continues to expand, the range of services that libraries can provide to users will continue to grow. With the increased development of mobile technology, librarians need to stay abreast of these new developments in order to remain relevant. I hope that you find this book a helpful resource as you look for ideas on how you can provide mobile services and resources to your users.

Acknowledgments

I would like to thank my colleagues, Greg Decker, Randall Myers, Helen Bischoff, and Michele Ruth, for the many conversations we have had regarding mobile technology and the encouragement they have provided me in pursuing this project. I would also like to thank my wonderful friends Linda and Gayla for constantly keeping me on my toes with questions about their mobile devices. Most of all, I would like to thank my wonderful wife, Julia, whose support and encouragement helped make this project possible. Finally, I would like to thank my editor, Sandy Wood, for her patience and direction throughout this project.

Why Mobile Matters

TECHNOLOGICAL DEVELOPMENT IN MOBILE COMPUTING has increased dramatically in a short period of time. There is now a wide array of mobile devices across a varying range of mobile operating systems that are changing the way people access information and interact with the world around them. As mobile technology continues to become ingrained in the collective consciousness of society, libraries and librarians need to make their information and services available in a mobile-optimized format to meet the changing needs of users. Mobile technology has become an important aspect in business, as companies see the benefits and potential for additional revenue options that mobile provides. With the rapid expansion of mobile technology, society will come to expect access to information in a format optimized for any device. The main focus of this chapter is the expansion of mobile technology in a broader context and how it has become an important focus of businesses.

Mobile Device Penetration

On April 3, 1973, the first call was made from a cell phone. It was made by Martin Cooper, a vice president and division manager at Motorola, to the head of research at Bell

Labs at a press conference from his office in New York. The phone used to make this call was the DynaTac, which had a less-than-thirty-minute battery life and took ten hours to recharge (Cheng 2013). The mobile phone has evolved significantly since that first call was made, as has access to it. More than forty years later, mobile device ownership, specifically mobile phone ownership, has reached a point where a majority of consumers across the globe now own such a device. According to *The Mobile Consumer: A Global Snapshot*, a report by the Neilson Company, nearly 94 percent of consumers over the age of sixteen own a mobile phone in the United States. Mobile phone ownership globally breaks down as follows:

- Australia, 86 percent
- Brazil, 84 percent
- China, 89 percent
- India, 81 percent
- Italy, 97 percent
- Russia, 98 percent
- South Korea, 99 percent
- United Kingdom, 97 percent (Neilson Company 2013)

These statistics show that mobile phone ownership is prevalent in both developed and high-growth economies.

To further illustrate the rapid expansion of access to mobile phones, consider a report from the United Nations on global sanitation. According to the United Nations, of the world's seven billion people, six billion have access to a mobile phone, while only 4.5 billion have access to toilets or latrines (United Nations 2013). Essentially, more people in the world today have access to a mobile phone than to proper sanitation. While this statistic may seem a little disturbing, it shows just how important access to mobile phones has become globally. Growing at an even greater rate is the access and ownership of smartphones, which are rapidly changing how we interact with and connect to the world around us.

Smartphones

Gone are the days of the big, clunky mobile phone that some of us may have been introduced to by Zack Morris on the television show *Saved by the Bell*, or the one used by Chris Kattan and Will Ferrell in the comedy *A Night at the Roxbury*. In its place is a mobile device that has evolved to be not only a phone but a small-screen mobile computing device that also makes phone calls—or what we simply refer to as a smartphone. *The Merriam-Webster Dictionary* defines a smartphone as "a cell phone that includes additional software functions (as e-mail or an Internet browser)." However, that seems a rather simplistic definition given the capabilities of smartphones. A more in-depth definition of a smartphone is a mobile phone that has highly advanced features. These features include a touch screen, Wi-Fi connectivity, Web browsing, built-in applications, and the ability to run third-party applications and function on advanced mobile operating systems such as Android or iOS. The first time the term *smartphone* was used was in 1997 in reference to the Ericsson GS88 (Kovach 2011). Although the Ericsson GS88 was the first phone to be referred to as a smartphone, the IBM Simon is considered the first such device. The IBM Simon was the first mobile phone to have a touchscreen and the ability to send and receive e-mails. Initially, smartphones were geared more toward the business sector, but they have since become widely available to the general public.

Smartphone ownership continues to drive the current mobile landscape. In the United States, smartphone penetration has reached an important milestone. The end of 2012 marked the first time that smartphone ownership gained a majority of the mobile market share. During that time, smartphone ownership in the United States accounted for 54 percent of the mobile market. That equates to 125.9 million smartphone owners over the age of thirteen, an increase of 29 percent from 2011 and a 99 percent increase from 2009. Not only have smartphones gained a majority of the mobile market share, but they now account for 72 percent of all newly acquired devices (comScore 2013). On a global scale, smartphone ownership varies dramatically, breaking down as follows:

- Australia, 65 percent
- Brazil, 36 percent
- China, 65 percent
- India, 10 percent
- Italy, 62 percent
- Russia, 37 percent
- South Korea, 67 percent
- United Kingdom, 61 percent (Neilson Company 2013)

These numbers show that although mobile phone ownership in some countries is high, there is sometimes a significant difference in smartphone ownership. One notable case is India, where mobile phone ownership is 81 percent but smartphone ownership is 10 percent.

Although smartphones have been around since 1997, it was not until Apple released the iPhone in 2007 that the mobile phone market began to shift. Since the development and release of the first iPhone, we have seen an explosion in the number of smartphones available to consumers. With the expansion of smartphones in the United States has come the development of a variety of mobile operating systems, including Apple's iOS and Google's Android. These mobile operating systems have transformed our mobile phones into powerful small-screen computing devices that range in screen size from three and a half inches to a little more than five inches. Looking at the technology adoption lifecycle (figure 1.1), smartphone penetration in the United States has now crossed into the "late majority."

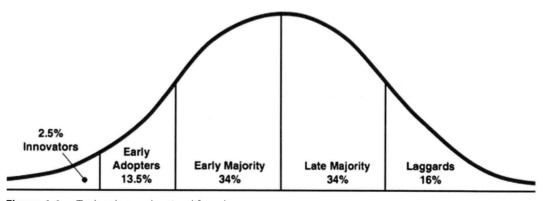

Figure 1.1. Technology adoption lifecycle.

The technology adoption lifecycle is a sociological model that was developed by Joe Bohlen, George Beal, and Everett Rogers at Iowa State University. The original intent of their research was to track the adoption of new strains of seed potatoes among farmers in the United States (Moore 2002). Everett Rogers later generalized the model in his book *Diffusion of Innovations* to describe how new ideas and technologies spread in different societies and cultures. In *Diffusion of Innovations*, diffusion is described as a process in which an innovation is communicated through certain channels over time among members of a society. An innovation, according to Rogers, is an idea, practice, or object that an individual or society perceives as new (Rogers 1982).

Within the technology adoption lifecycle, there are five categories of adopters that will ultimately determine whether a technology is accepted or rejected. These five categories are innovators, early adopters, early majority, late majority, and laggards. These categories are based on the level of innovativeness of members of society. Rogers describes innovativeness as the "degree to which an individual or other unit of adoption is relatively earlier in adopting new ideas than the other members of a social system" (Rogers 1982, 22). Innovators make up a very small portion of adopters (2.5 percent), but they are an essential part of technology adoption. This group typically pursues new technology progressively. Technology is a central interest in their lives, and they are often quick to adopt technology regardless of its function because they are fascinated by technology itself. Rogers describes this group as venturous. Following the innovators are the early adopters, who make up 13.5 percent of adopters. This group, like innovators, buys into new technology concepts early in the cycle. However, unlike innovators, they are not technologists. Rather, they are individuals who are able to imagine, understand, and appreciate the benefits of new technological advances. As a group, they have opinion leadership, and they are often considered the "people to check with" when considering a new type of technology. The next group, the early majority, adopts new technologies before the average member of society, but they are more deliberate in their decision making. They want to ensure that the technology is not just a passing fad before they invest in it. They make up 34 percent of the adopters. Also making up 34 percent are the late majority. Members of this group tend to be more skeptical about technology. They adopt new technologies after the average member of society, and they may do so out of economic necessity and in response to increased pressure from peers. The last group to adopt technology is the laggards. They typically do not have much to do with technology, and when they do adopt something, it may have already been superseded by a new technology currently being used by the innovators. This group accounts for 16 percent of adopters (Rogers 1982; Moore 2002). The adoption rate of technology among these groups will determine whether a new technology is a success or a failure. The smartphone has been a huge success, and its ownership among consumers is expected to rise steadily. In fact, it is projected that 80 percent of the population in the United States will own a smartphone by 2015 (Goldman 2010).

Tablets

Like smartphones, tablet computers are experiencing a substantial growth among consumers in the United States. However, they have achieved a level of adoption in a significantly shorter time than it took smartphones when they were initially introduced. Tablet computers, simply referred to as tablets, are general-purpose portable computers that are contained in a single touch-screen panel. Tablets have not been around nearly as long as smartphones. Microsoft first made the term *tablet* popular back in 2001. Then Microsoft CEO Bill Gates was so certain that tablets were the future that he stated in an interview with CNN, "The tablet takes cutting-edge PC technology and makes it available whenever you want it, which is why I'm already using a tablet as my everyday computer. . . . It's a PC that is virtually without limits—and within five years I predict it will be the most popular form of PC sold in America." Microsoft went about producing tablets, but other than in a few specialized sectors, the tablet market never really took off due to concerns from consumers. Some of those concerns were that the price for tablets were a premium over traditional notebooks, that they ran on an operating system that was designed around the use of a keyboard and mouse, and that they required the use of an input device such as a stylus (Griffey 2012). As a result, the tablet market died down until 2010 when Apple introduced the iPad.

Since the introduction of the iPad, tablet ownership has increased steadily and has ushered in what former Apple CEO Steve Jobs referred to as the "post-PC era." In fact, the iPad became the fastest selling non-phone electronic product ever, with more than three million units sold within the first eighty days of release (Melloy 2010). According to the Pew Internet and American Life Project, in May 2010 tablet ownership in the United States stood at 3 percent of the population eighteen years of age and older. As of May 2013, that number has increased to 34 percent, almost double the figure from May 2012, which was 18 percent (Pew Internet and American Life Project 2013). The growth of tablet ownership is expected to continue, as many analysts expect the sale of tablets to outpace the sale of desktop and portable personal computers within the next few years.

Tablets have also been making their way into the field of education. Not only are individual consumers seeing the benefits of tablets, but some school districts and higher education institutions are starting to implement and look at ways that tablets can be injected into the curriculum. Brookfield High School in Connecticut, Burlington High School near Boston, and Woodford County High School in Kentucky are among some of the schools that are infusing iPads into their curriculum. In 2011, Apple reported there were more than six hundred school districts that had launched "one-to-one" programs where at least one classroom is getting iPads for each student to use throughout the day (Associated Press 2011). Higher education institutions such as Lynn University and Arkansas State University are either providing all of their incoming freshmen with an iPad or requiring that students acquire one shortly after arriving on campus. Although Bill Gates was a few years off in his prediction, his outlook was correct. Tablets are poised to become the most popular form of computer sold in the United States. The adoption of tablets has just passed into the stage of the early majority on the technology adoption lifecycle, but given their quick ascent with the revitalization of the tablet market, the potential for growth is extremely promising. Although tablets have yet to reach the popularity of smartphones, it is worth mentioning again that they have attained a much quicker rate of adoption than smartphones. Adoption has also extended beyond the reach of individual consumers and into the field of education, as school districts and higher education institutions begin to see the educational benefits of these mobile devices.

E-readers

An e-reader is another popular mobile device among consumers. An e-reader is primarily used to read digital copies of books, magazines, journals, and other digital content. They may have the ability to search the Web, but they are not built on an advanced mobile operating system like smartphones and tablets. Although e-readers have not quite reached the popularity of smartphones and tablets, they have seen a steady growth over the last several years. According to the Pew Internet and American Life Project, 19 percent of Americans over the age of eighteen owned an e-reading device as of November 2012 (Pew Internet and American Life Project 2012a). This represents an increase in ownership of 9 percent over December 2011.

As with tablets, e-reader ownership is currently in the early majority adoption stage of the technology adoption lifecycle. Despite this similarity to tablets, e-readers do not appear to be growing at the same rate, nor are they expected to. While tablet ownership rose during 2012, e-reader ownership remained relatively stagnant. Although the growth of e-reader ownership has not kept pace with the growth of smartphones and tablets, there has been an increase in the number of e-books being read by the U.S. population.

According to the Pew Internet and American Life Project, the percentage of Americans age sixteen and older that read an e-book in 2012 was 23 percent. That is an increase over the previous year, when the percentage of Americans who read an e-book was 16 percent. The Pew Internet and American Life Project found during that same time period that the percentage of Americans reading print books had decreased from 72 percent in 2011 to 67 percent in 2012 (Pew Internet and American Life Project 2012a). So while e-reader ownership appears to be leveling out at the present, e-book reading is continuing to increase. This can most likely be attributed to companies such as Amazon and Barnes and Noble, both of whom sell e-readers, developing mobile applications for smartphones and tablets for consumers to access their digital content. While this may hurt the sale of e-readers, it allows those companies to continue to profit off of the sale of e-books and deliver digital content to consumers through the mobile devices that they are already using. Apple got in on the sale of e-books and other digital reading content with the development of the iBooks Store, whose release coincided with that of the iPad in 2010.

As a result of the rapid expansion of mobile technologies, the focus of companies such as Google, Facebook, and Apple has shifted, and it will be exciting to see what new mobile technologies they have in store for us in the near future.

Mobile, Business, and the Consumer

The rapid rise and expansion of the mobile platform can be traced back to the introduction and release of the iPhone in 2007. The iPhone was a device that provided consumers with a mobile computer that fit right into their pockets. Many of the same activities associated with desktop computers, such as Web browsing, image and video creation, as well as other tasks, were now possible within the mobile environment. It was no longer about using your mobile phone just to make phone calls and send text messages. The iPhone was a device that enabled consumers to constantly be connected to the world around them over a cellular network. It dramatically transformed what they would expect from future generations of mobile devices. At the time of the iPhone's release, the late Steve Jobs, cofounder and then CEO of Apple, said, "Every once in a while a revolutionary product comes along that changes everything" (Honan 2007). It did change things. It changed consumer expectations; it changed the information consumption behaviors of people; and it opened up a new medium that businesses could tap into. Apple provided a successful blueprint for the smartphone, and later the tablet computer, that many companies would follow. With the release of the iPhone and other smartphone devices from leading mobile phone manufacturers such as Samsung, businesses now had to shift their strategies to determine the best ways to reach consumers in the mobile environment.

Apple, in 2008, would release the App Store, and shortly thereafter would open up their platform to third-party developers through the development and release of a native software development kit (SDK). Third-party applications were not initially supported on the iPhone. The reason is that Steve Jobs felt that developers could use Web 2.0 technologies to build Web applications that behaved like native applications. Google would follow suit with the development and release of an SDK for the Android mobile operating system and their app store, the Android Market (now known as Google Play). Armed with these SDKs and mobile platforms, developers could begin making native applications. This was an opportunity that businesses could seize. Companies interested in targeting specific mobile platforms, such as iOS and Android, could enlist the skills of their information technology departments or reach out to third-party developers to build native applications. The mobile environment was another avenue of potential profit. Here was the chance to reach consumers through advertising, develop convenient and efficient ways for consumers to shop from their mobile devices, and provide mobile banking access, among many other possibilities. Thus companies began incorporating a mobile strategy into their business models, and some even decided on a mobile-first strategy. The mobile-first strategy involves focusing on mobile as the main building block for a business. Regardless of whether companies are developing native applications or mobile advertising campaigns, one thing is certain: they have made mobile a priority.

Mobile devices, smartphones in particular, were able to create a bridge to two previously unconnected industries: wireless networks and personal computing. This bridge has created a monumental opportunity for wireless carriers (such as AT&T and Verizon) and personal computing companies (such as Apple and Google) to reap the benefits in the form of revenue and profits. On a global scale, the nine hundred wireless carriers combine to take in more than $1.3 trillion in revenue each year. However, individual mobile device manufacturers, most notably Apple, are able to seize more profit. These device manufacturers have capitalized on profits by bringing personal computing into the mobile environment through devices like the iPhone and the Samsung Galaxy smartphone. This has greatly increased their companies' value and capabilities. A perfect example of profitability would be the average wholesale price of a mobile phone in 2007 and the change in pricing since then. In 2007, the year the iPhone was released, the average price of a mobile phone was around $120 and declining. Many analysts attributed this to market saturation; everyone who could afford a mobile phone owned one. However, since the release of the iPhone and various other smartphone devices, mobile handset prices have increased by more than 50 percent, and revenue from these sales has doubled (Regalado 2013). With the dramatic growth in mobile usage, coupled with personal computing becoming a serious component of the mobile environment, companies now have an additional medium to get their message to consumers, and one way that companies are doing just that is through mobile advertising.

According to the Mobile Consumer Habits study released by Jumio Incorporated, 72 percent of consumers responded that a majority of time they are within five feet of their smartphones (Davis 2013). Given this fact, it is no wonder that companies are investing in mobile advertising. While still a relatively young practice, mobile advertising is starting to expand as more and more companies develop effective means to reach users in the mobile environment.

So what is mobile advertising, and what does it encompass? Although many people might think mobile advertising refers to mobile banner ads or mobile search results—and it does—mobile advertising involves more than just these methods. It now involves many different formats and interactive experiences. One type of advertising mechanism that mobile has made possible is location-based advertising. Location-based advertising uses the positional services of mobile devices to target consumers based on their geographic location (Dhar and Varshney 2011). This allows businesses to create local mobile advertising. Companies can get offers in front of consumers at the right moment. It also enables businesses to provide a new level of relevance in mobile offers to consumers, giving them what they need, when they need it, and where they need it (Mobile Advertising Hub 2013). Location-based advertising is valuable to businesses because it can provide insight into the actual behaviors of consumers through the use of both real-time and historical data that shows where actual customer transactions have occurred. This is just one tool that companies are using to reach consumers in the mobile environment. Companies are also expanding their mobile advertising tools to include different formats and components to match the ever-expanding capabilities of smartphones and other mobile devices.

Mobile advertising now includes more videos and interactive components. For example, the Discovery Channel promoted the show *Storm Chasers* with mobile ads that took over the speakers of mobile devices and made them vibrate to simulate the sounds and effects of a storm. Another example is the collaborative effort between Coca-Cola and Google in their mobile ad campaign "Buy the World a Coke." This campaign, optimized for social media, asked people if they would like to send a free coke to someone else around the world. The free coke was then sent to a specially outfitted Coca-Cola vending machine in cities around the world. Recipients could record a video thanking the sender for the free coke (Mobile Advertising Hub 2013). These are just two examples of how companies are creating more interactive components to their mobile advertising campaigns in a variety of different formats.

Analysts are projecting that mobile advertising has the potential for tremendous growth. Aiding this potential are the attractive features of mobile devices, including the following:

- Portability
- Personalization and instant access
- Mobility and wireless Internet connectivity
- Location awareness
- Context awareness (Dhar and Varshney 2011)

These features, as well as the increased adoption of smartphones and other mobile devices, have created another platform for businesses to use for advertising.

Despite the potential for revenue from mobile advertising, there appears to be a disconnect in the business world. Although mobile advertising currently brings in $9 billion, a pretty healthy sum, most publications state that mobile advertising *only* accounts for $9 billion. This qualification reflects the tremendous potential of mobile advertising revenue and illustrates that the potential is not anywhere close to being met. This could be because many companies—and Internet companies specifically—were not prepared for the rapid shift of online activity from computers to smartphones and tablet computers. One such example is Facebook. During the initial public offering (IPO) of their stock, the company reported that they were not making any significant revenue from their mobile app or website. Essentially, their revenue from mobile advertising was close to zero. Given that a large percentage of their monthly audience was coming from mobile devices, and that 23 percent of the time that Americans spend on mobile apps is devoted to Facebook, this was problematic (Regalado 2013). In an interview with *Forbes*, Sense Networks CEO David Petersen provided further insight into the problem with mobile advertising revenue. He stated that "studies are showing that mobile is on the wrong side of a monetization gap. While the average consumer now spends a significant percentage of their time consuming media through mobile, the percent of advertising budgets spent in the category is lagging well behind" (Olenski 2013).

Notwithstanding the challenges of mobile advertising, there is much for businesses to be excited about. Even though Facebook had no significant income from mobile advertising during their IPO, they began to make significant steps in the right direction. During the last three months of 2012, Facebook's mobile advertising revenue climbed to $305 million. Although still behind Google's mobile ad revenue of $2.2 billion in 2012 (Hof 2013), Facebook has had success. Many companies are starting to see the potential for mobile advertising revenue. As a result, spending on mobile advertising is expected to increase dramatically over the next several years. Spending on mobile advertising in 2012 was $8.41 billion, and it is expected to climb to more than $37 billion by 2016 (Jones 2013). This is good news for the likes of Google and Facebook, as they are the firms best positioned to profit from this increased spending.

Another notable way that smartphones and other mobile devices are impacting businesses is through mobile shopping. The amount of time that smartphone users spent on online retail grew 385 percent from February 2010 to February 2013, an increase from 2.7 billion minutes to 12.9 billion minutes a year. As of March 2013, smartphone and tablet computers accounted for 48 percent of the time spent on online retail (Siwicki 2013). In addition to time, consumers are spending more money when shopping from their mobile device. In 2012, consumers spent more than $25 billion in online purchases using their mobile devices. This amounts to an increase of 81 percent over 2011. Research firm eMarketer expects that number to increase to $87 billion by 2016, which would equal more than 27 percent of all e-commerce transactions (Musil 2013).

Smartphones have enabled consumers to become better and smarter shoppers, or at the very least more informed shoppers. Not only have mobile devices altered consumer behavior with online retail, but these devices have also altered consumers' shopping behaviors while they are at physical store locations. A study done in conjunction with the Google Shopper Marketing Agency Council and M/A/R/C Research examined the ways smartphone owners are using their devices. They found that 84 percent use their devices in stores. The study also found that 90 percent of smartphone shoppers use their device for preshopping activities like the following:

- Finding the location of a store (58 percent)
- Finding hours (57 percent)
- Making price comparisons (44 percent)
- Finding promotional offers (44 percent)
- Browsing (43 percent)
- Finding where specific products are sold (32 percent)
- Finding product information (31 percent)
- Finding product availability in store (31 percent)
- Reading product reviews (30 percent)
- Making purchases (19 percent) (Google 2013)

Nearly half of consumers that use their smartphones while shopping in store spend fifteen minutes or more on them per visit. The most common activity when shopping in a store is price comparison, which is made easy with the use of mobile applications like Amazon Price Check and Red Laser. These types of native applications let consumers scan the barcode of an item and compare the price with other retailers both online and in the near vicinity. Price comparison is often used with big-ticket items such as appliances and electronics. A way that some companies are engaging smartphone-equipped consumers is through the use of QR codes. An example is Best Buy. On many of their products, Best Buy has a QR code so consumers can link to their mobile website and get more information on a particular product and access customer reviews.

A downside for brick-and-mortar businesses is that they can often become showrooms for online retailers to which they are in no way connected. Best Buy, again, is a perfect example, and they have often been referred to as "Amazon's Showroom"—meaning that they serve as a place where consumers can come to check out items in the store and then order them online at a better price. To combat situations such as this, Best Buy has begun offering price matching, which is a strong deterrent to the showroom problem. Regardless of the ramifications, businesses are adapting to the mobile shopper and finding ways to engage them, whether they are using their mobile devices for online retail or while in the store. Consumers are starting to rely more on mobile shopping for various reasons. Chief among them is that using a smartphone saves time. Other reasons that consumers have given are that it saves them money and that it makes their lives easier.

There are many more significant developments that have been occurring in relation to mobile technologies and business. More and more companies are trying to gain a share of the mobile handset market, where Apple and Samsung currently dominate. Companies like Google, Amazon, and Microsoft are making a huge push to undercut the dominance of Apple in the tablet market. In this realm, Amazon appears to be abandoning the concept of manufacturing a stand-alone e-reading device in favor of moving their Kindle line into the tablet market, and they have had some success. Other companies, such as Barnes and Noble, have not had the success enjoyed by Apple and Amazon. As a result, they have scaled back their efforts in the tablet market.

Headway has been made in a variety of service areas to provide mobile access to consumers. One such service is mobile banking. Banks are now providing their customers with mobile applications and websites that make banking more convenient. Customers can check the balances of their accounts and transfer money, and some banks have even added the feature of check deposits from mobile devices. Customers are able to do this by snapping a picture of a check and submitting it to their bank through an app.

Mobile acquisitions have been a big development in business as well, especially in the technology industry. For example, Facebook acquired Instagram, the popular photo application, for $1 billion. Apple and Google are also acquiring smaller mobile-focused businesses to fold into and enhance their mobile ecosystems. Google acquired Waze for $1 billion in June 2013. Waze is a GPS-enabled navigation application that uses turn-by-turn navigation as well as user-submitted travel times and routes. Google has begun integrating real-time Waze user traffic reports into the Google Maps iOS and Android applications. The list goes on. It is safe to say that mobile technologies have provided businesses with a unique opportunity and a few challenges as well. As businesses continue to focus on reaching consumers in the mobile environment, they need to be aware of what types of activities consumers are using their mobile devices for. According to *The Mobile Consumer: A Global Snapshot*, Americans use their mobile devices, and their smartphones in particular, for the following activities:

- Text messaging/SMS (86 percent)
- E-mail (75 percent)
- Instant messaging (28 percent)
- Social networking (63 percent)
- Streaming online music (38 percent)
- Video/mobile TV (28 percent)
- Applications (62 percent)
- Web browsing (82 percent)
- Mobile shopping (30 percent)
- Mobile banking (38 percent)
- Location-based services/GPS (48 percent)
- Barcode or QR scanning (24 percent)
- NFC/mobile wallet (3 percent) (Neilson Company 2013)

Armed with these insights, businesses can develop strategies to reach consumers effectively in the mobile environment. With the increasing adoption of mobile devices, it is imperative for businesses to give mobile adequate attention, as consumers are expecting more and more as the capabilities of these devices continue to expand.

⊚ Key Points

This chapter has focused on the rapid expansion of mobile technologies and how the rapid development in mobile computing has affected businesses.

- Mobile technology is changing how people access information and interact with the world around them.
- Adoption of mobile devices like smartphones and tablets has seen a significant increase since the inception of the iPhone and iPad.
- Businesses like Facebook are seeing the potential for revenue that mobile provides as more and more users access information on their mobile devices.

Now that you have an understanding of the overall importance of mobile technology, the rest of this book will focus on the importance and implementation of mobile technology within libraries.

⊚ References

Associated Press. 2011. "Many U.S. Schools Adding iPads, Trimming Textbooks." *USA Today*, September 2. http://usatoday30.usatoday.com/news/education/story/2011-09-03/Many-US -schools-adding-iPads-trimming-textbooks/50251238/1.

Cheng, R. 2013. "The First Call from a Cell Phone Was Made 40 Years Ago Today." *CNET*, April 3. http://news.cnet.com/8301-1035_3-57577704-94/the-first-call-from-a-cell-phone-was -made-40-years-ago-today/.

comScore. 2013. *2013 Mobile Future in Focus*. Reston, VA.

Davis, J. 2013. "Americans Can't Put Down Their Smartphones, Even during Sex." Jumio, July 11. http://www.jumio.com/2013/07/americans-cant-put-down-their-smartphones-even -during-sex/.

Dhar, Subhankar, and Upkar Varshney. 2011. "Challenges and Business Models for Mobile Loca- tion-Based Services and Advertising." *Communications of the ACM* 54, no. 5 (May): 121–28.

Goldman, D. 2010. "Your Smartphone Will Run Your Life." *CNN*, October 19. http://money.cnn .com/2010/10/19/technology/smartphones/index.htm.

Google. 2013. "How Mobile Is Transforming the Shopping Experience in Stores." April. http:// www.google.com/think/research-studies/mobile-in-store.html.

Griffey, Jason. 2012. "The Rise of the Tablet." *Library Technology Reports* 48, no. 3 (April): 7–13.

Hof, Robert. 2013. "How Facebook Slew the Mobile Monster." *MIT Technology Review* 116, no. 3 (March): 75.

Honan, M. 2007. "Apple Unveils iPhone." *Macworld*, January 9. http://www.macworld.com/ article/1054769/iphone.html.

Jones, C. 2013. "Mobile Ad Spending Forecast to Increase 4X over the Next 4 Years." *Forbes*, Janu- ary 4. http://www.forbes.com/sites/chuckjones/2013/01/04/mobile-ad-spending-forecast-to -increase-4x-over-the-next-4-years/.

Kovach, S. 2011. "Here Are All the Smartphone Features You Love So Much and Who Had Them First." *Business Insider*, August 12. http://www.businessinsider.com/smartphone-firsts -2011-8?op=1.

Melloy, J. 2010. "iPad Adoption Rate Fastest Ever, Passing DVD Player." *CNBC*, October 4. http://www.cnbc.com/id/39501308.

Mobile Advertising Hub. 2013. "What Is Mobile Advertising? More Than You Think!" http:// mobileadvertisinghub.com/what-is-mobile-advertising-more-than-you-think/.

Moore, Geoffrey. 2002. *Crossing the Chasm: Marketing and Selling Disruptive Products to Main- stream Customers*. New York: HarperBusiness Essentials.

Musil, S. 2013. "Shopping via Mobile Devices Increased 81 Percent in 2012." *CNET*, Janu- ary 9. http://news.cnet.com/8301-1023_3-57563184-93/shopping-via-mobile-devices-in creased-81-percent-in-2012/.

Neilson Company. 2013. *The Mobile Consumer: A Global Snapshot*. New York.

Olenski, S. 2013. "Is Location Based Advertising the Future of Mobile Marketing and Mobile Advertising?" *Forbes*, January 17. http://www.forbes.com/sites/marketshare/2013/01/17/is -location-based-advertising-the-future-of-mobile-marketing-and-mobile-advertising/.

Pew Internet and American Life Project. 2012a. "E-book Reading Jumps; Print Book Reading Declines." December 27. http://libraries.pewinternet.org/files/legacy-pdf/PIP_Reading%20 and%20ebooks_12.27.pdf.

———. 2012b. "Tablet and E-book Reader Ownership Nearly Double over the Holiday Gift- Giving Period." January 23. http://libraries.pewinternet.org/2012/01/23/tablet-and-e-book -reader-ownership-nearly-double-over-the-holiday-gift-giving-period/.

———. 2013. "Tablet Ownership 2013." June 10. http://www.pewinternet.org/files/old-media/ Files/Reports/2013/PIP_Tablet%20ownership%202013.pdf.

Regalado, Antonio. 2013. "Making Money in Mobile." *MIT Technology Review* 116, no. 3 (March): 1–3.

Rogers, Everett. 1982. *Diffusion of Innovations*. New York: Free Press.

Siwicki, B. 2013. "Online Shopping Becomes Increasingly Mobile." *Internet Retailer*, May 15. http://www.internetretailer.com/2013/05/15/online-shopping-becomes-increasingly-mobile.

United Nations. 2013. "Deputy UN Chief Calls for Urgent Action to Tackle Global Sanitation Crisis." March 21. http://www.un.org/apps/news/story.asp?NewsID=44452.

CHAPTER 2

User Expectations and the Impact of Mobile Technologies on Libraries

---

IN THIS CHAPTER

▷ User expectations of mobile devices

▷ The impact of mobile technology on library services

▷ User preference regarding mobile websites and native applications

---

AS THE CAPABILITIES OF MOBILE DEVICES CONTINUE to expand, so do the expectations of users. Mobile users expect their devices to have high-quality hardware and software. As the adoption of mobile rises, users will expect to perform essential tasks using their mobile devices. When interacting with their devices, the expectation is that websites will be user friendly and optimized for viewing. The rapid expansion of mobile technology has had a profound impact on library services. As a result, libraries are developing and restructuring services to meet the needs and expectations of mobile users.

User Expectations

With the introduction of new technologies, it is inevitable that users will begin to see the possibilities and that their expectations will increase as the technology matures. Mobile technology has reached that point. The introduction of the iPhone provided users with a window through which to see the potential of mobile technology. Users gained access to a wealth of information in the palm of their hand. Smartphones were starting to be built around an operating system designed specifically for the mobile environment, which had tremendous capabilities. However, the one big issue was that there were very few companies ready for the mobile revolution that the iPhone set off. Additionally, there was very little of the Web that was mobile friendly. But now mobile technology and services are a core part of business and organizational strategies, as the adoption of the technology continues to expand. With this expansion comes increased expectations from users. Now that users are aware of what mobile devices are capable of, they expect a certain experience that makes their lives more efficient and user friendly. Additionally, they expect their mobile devices to continue to push the envelope. This means bigger screen sizes, high-definition displays, faster processors, better cameras, and enhancements to the mobile operating systems, just to name a few. User expectations are markedly different than they were in 2007, and those expectations will continue to shift as the capabilities of mobile technology continue to expand.

User expectations regarding mobile devices can be divided into two categories: devices and user experience. Expectations for devices include what users expect from their mobile hardware and software. User experience expectations involve how users are interacting with their mobile device. Users want to have a good experience when they are using a native application or when they are using a mobile website. To illustrate the expectations that users have, consider the expanding specifications of iPhones and Android-powered smartphones. The specifications for the first iPhone were:

- 3.5-inch (diagonal) widescreen multi-touch display
- 480-by-320-pixel resolution at 163 pixels per inch (ppi)
- 2.0-megapixel camera
- Internal storage options of 4 GB or 8 GB, with a 16 GB option added later
- Talk time of up to eight hours
- Internet use of up to six hours
- Up to 250 hours of standby
- Video playback for up to seven hours
- Audio playback for up to twenty-four hours
- 2G wireless network
- 4.8 ounces in weight (Apple 2010)

Those were very good specifications at the time of its release in 2007, but like any lasting technology, there have been significant improvements since then. There have currently been eight versions of the iPhone, the most recent being the iPhone 6 and 6Plus. There have been many features and functionalities added to the iPhone since 2007. The iPhone 6 is loaded with the following specifications:

- Retina display (high definition)
- 4.7-inch (diagonal) LED-backlit widescreen multi-touch display
- 1134-by-750-pixel resolution at 326 pixel per inch (ppi)
- 1400:1 contrast ratio
- Internal storage options of 16 GB, 64 GB, and 128 GB
- 8-megapixel iSight camera
- TouchID
- Panorama
- HD video recording (1080p) at 30 fps or 60 fps

- Slo-mo video at 120 fps or 240 fps
- Autofocus with focus pixels
- Tap to focus video or still images
- Improved face detection in video or still images
- True-tone flash
- Photo and video geotagging
- Talk time of up to fourteen hours
- Internet use of up to ten hours on 3G, up to ten hours on LTE, and eleven hours over Wi-Fi
- Up to 250 hours of standby
- Video playback for up to eleven hours
- Audio playback for up to fifty hours
- 3G and 4G wireless networks and Long-Term Evolution (LTE)
- A7 chip with 64-bit architecture
- M8 motion coprocessor
- 4.55 ounces in weight (Apple 2014)

As you can see, the iPhone has changed in some significant ways since it was first introduced. So have the specifications offered on the flagship Android smartphones. The HTC Dream was the first smartphone to be released using the Android operating system. In 2008, it was equipped with the following specifications:

- 3.2 LCD touchscreen display
- 480-by-320-pixel resolution at 180 pixels per inch (ppi)
- 3.15-megapixel camera with autofocus
- 528 MHz Qualcomm Processor
- Internal storage of 256 MB that is expandable to 16 GB with a microSD card
- QWERTY keyboard
- Up to 406 hours of standby
- Talk time up to five hours and twenty minutes
- 5.6 ounces in weight (Chan 2009)

The HTC Dream has since been replaced by a line of successors from HTC, but the Android mobile operating systems continues to thrive. Android is currently the market leader in the mobile operating system arena. The current Android line that is seen as a direct competitor to Apple's iPhone is the Samsung Galaxy series, and the most recent Galaxy release is the Alpha. The specifications for the Galaxy S5 include:

- Full HD Super AMOLED (1920 x 1080) display, 432 pixels per inch (ppi)
- 5.1-inch touchscreen display
- 2.5 GHz Quad-Core processor
- 16-megapixel autofocus camera with Phase Detection
- Front-facing 2-megapixel camera, full HD recording at thirty frames per second with zero shutter lag, backside illuminating sensor
- A variety of camera options that include Drama Shoot, 360 Photo, Eraser, Night, HDR, and Panorama

- Internal storage options of 16 GB and 32 GB plus the option to expand the memory to 128 GB with a microSD card
- Near field communication (NFC)
- Full HD video record capability
- Talk time up to twenty-one hours
- Up to 390 hours standby
- Audio playback up to sixty-seven hours
- 5.11 ounces in weight (Samsung 2014)

Whether it is an iPhone or an Android phone, smartphones and other mobile devices have vastly improved since they entered into the mainstream.

It may be the case that these devices have progressed as a natural evolution of technology. But while that is part of the reason, technology continues to progress because users expect it to. Smartphones and other mobile devices are equipped with a lot of features that would have seemed somewhat unbelievable just ten years ago. However, despite the many advances, users are constantly complaining about some software or hardware feature that is missing, specifically in smartphones. Once a new product is launched, users are already beginning to think about how the next iteration of that device can be improved. Users expect a lot from their mobile devices because they have seen what they are capable of. Mobile device makers, such as Apple and Samsung, must heed what users want and in some way meet expectations in order to stay competitive in the ever-expanding mobile market.

Given the capabilities of mobile devices and what user expectations are in regard to the physical device, there are also certain expectations when it comes to the user experience. Along with expecting premium hardware and software specifications from their physical devices, users also expect that their experience will be user friendly. The user experience can be an important factor influencing what device a user chooses. Not only do major device manufacturers like Apple and Samsung have to be concerned with technical specifications, but they also have to be mindful of things like navigation control. Mobile devices can have the best technical specifications, but if they are difficult to navigate, then it does not matter. Developers also need to be aware of the user experience when they are developing for the mobile environment.

As mobile technology progresses and becomes further ingrained in our culture, users expect more. Expectations now are quite different than they were even a few years ago. There is no longer the willingness to put up with clunky user experiences, especially when it comes to mobile websites and native applications. Take, for example, the shifting expectations of mobile users from 2009 to 2011. In 2009, 58 percent of users expected a website to load just as quickly as it would on a desktop computer. In 2011, the percentage of mobile users who had this expectation stood at 71 percent, which could be attributed to the proliferation of more robust Wi-Fi networks (Bixby 2011). Even more striking is the increase of mobile users who would leave a mobile website after waiting five seconds for a page to load. In 2009, 20 percent of mobile users would leave after five seconds. In 2011, that number jumped to 74 percent (Bixby 2011). Overall, mobile users tend to be less tolerant and more demanding than desktop users.

Mobile users are just as demanding when it comes to applications. A survey of respondents from the United States, the United Kingdom, France, Germany, India, and Japan found that applications are expected to load at an even faster rate than mobile websites. The top response was that a mobile application should launch in two seconds. If users have a poor experience using a mobile application, 48 percent are less likely to use it again, 34 percent will switch to a competitor if one is available, and 31 percent will share their poor experience with others (Sterling 2013). If an application does not work correctly the first time, users will likely only give it one or two more chances. These statistics and insights illustrate that mobile users have high expectations of mobile websites and applications. It also implies that users expect there to be mobile websites and applications for them to access.

Impact of Mobile on Libraries

With the expansion of mobile technology comes the need and demand for access to information in a format suitable for mobile devices. Libraries have long been a beacon of information for users through various print and digital collections and formats. However, the mobile environment has presented a slew of new challenges and opportunities for libraries, just as it has for other organizations. Mobile users' expectations extend to library services. With more and more library users coming equipped with various mobile devices, libraries must be ready to meet the needs and expectations of these users.

The influx of mobile devices has had a profound impact on libraries. In some cases, this impact has meant offering new services or evaluating and planning how to extend current services into the mobile environment. Many libraries are seizing this exciting opportunity and beginning to explore various options to meet the needs and expectations of mobile users. One step many libraries are taking is to create a mobile interface for their websites or, at the very least, a mobile interface for their online public access catalog (OPAC). Some libraries are able to provide a mobile interface to their OPAC through their integrated library system (ILS) vendor. Examples of mobile library websites include the Orange County Library System in Orlando, Florida; Oregon State University Libraries in Corvallis, Oregon; and Worthington Libraries in Worthington, Ohio. Other libraries are looking to extend their mobile reach to specific mobile platforms through the development of native applications. One such library is the District of Columbia Public Library, which developed the first public library iPhone application in the United States and released it as open source code for other libraries to use.

The range of tasks users expect to be able to perform is growing, and as a result libraries are incorporating more and more features into mobile websites. Instead of offering the bare amount of information, such as contact information and library hours, library mobile websites are providing access to more information and resources. Take, for example, a study examining the items that academic libraries most frequently use on their mobile websites. The study found that these items were the most frequently used:

- Search link (86 percent)
- Hours (80 percent)
- Locations/maps (59 percent)
- Contact us/contact information (53 percent)
- Ask-a-Librarian (47 percent)
- News/events (32 percent)
- Personal account/renew (28 percent)
- Search box (25 percent)
- Research guide (by subject) (24 percent)

- Laptop/computer availability (18 percent)
- Study room reservation (11 percent)
- Feedback (11 percent)
- Social network (7 percent)
- FAQ/help (7 percent)
- Staff directory (7 percent)
- About us (5 percent)
- Course reserves (4 percent) (Kim 2013)

Additionally, libraries are eliciting feedback from users to determine what types of services and resources users want in a mobile library website. Kent State University students wanted:

- To use their mobile device to access research databases
- To read materials on course reserve
- To search the library catalog on a mobile device
- To request an item or place it on hold from their phone
- To have customizable options and personalized information from the library regarding their account and other services
- To be contacted by text message when a requested library item was available for pickup or when material was nearing its due date
- To receive text message reminders about upcoming library appointments
- To have options for customizing their mobile Web experience, such as being able to pick their favorite databases or choose their own top ten links to see on a mobile website
- To be able to refer to a library building guide and find an explanation of the call number system
- To have a live chat or text message exchange with a librarian about a research question or how to cite a source (Kim 2013)

Mobile devices have also opened up the possibility of offering new services and extending current ones. One area of library services that mobile has directly impacted is reference. Chat services can now be accessed by users on their mobile devices through mobile-friendly chat providers like LibraryH3lp. Texting a librarian is also a new service that some libraries have or are beginning to implement. In addition to offering more reference services, libraries are starting to circulate physical mobile devices such as tablets and e-readers. North Carolina State University Libraries and Concordia University Libraries in Montreal, Canada, are two examples that are lending tablets to users. North Carolina State University Libraries lends 42 iPads and 4 Google Nexus 7 tablets, and Concordia University Libraries lends 125 iPads to users. Hooksett Public Library in New Hampshire and the University of Louisville are lending e-readers. Hooksett Public Library offers a variety of different e-readers that their users can check out, including the following:

- Nook Classic
- Nook Color
- Nook Simple
- Nook HD 7"

- Sony Reader
- Kobo e-reader
- Kindle 3G Keyboard
- Kindle Fire
- Kindle Fire HD 7"
- Kindle Paperwhite (Hooksett Public Library 2014)

The University of Louisville offers eighteen Kindles for their users to check out. These are just a few examples of how mobile devices have impacted libraries and how libraries have adapted or offered new services to meet the needs and expectations of mobile users.

Despite the many opportunities that mobile devices offer for libraries, they also present various challenges. In terms of developing mobile interfaces and applications, libraries may not have the expertise on staff to tackle mobile development. There are budgetary concerns as well. Whether developing for mobile devices or acquiring them for circulation, the investment is not cheap and can be beyond the means of library budgets. However, despite all of the challenges, the fact remains that mobile technology has had, and will continue to have, a direct impact on libraries.

⑥ Key Points

Increasing developments in mobile technology and in the capabilities of mobile devices have dramatically changed user expectations. As a result, librarians are looking at ways to meet the expectations of mobile users through a variety of different means.

- Mobile user expectations are driving mobile device manufacturers to create devices that are built with high-quality hardware and software and developers to create mobile interfaces that function and are built with the user experience in mind.
- In light of the expansion of mobile technologies, libraries are looking at ways to expand services. Examples include embedding current services into the mobile environment, developing mobile interfaces, and lending mobile devices to users.

Libraries must now contend with incorporating mobile technologies into their services, which can seem like an overwhelming task given the wide variety of devices available. In the next chapter, this book discusses how libraries can go about deciding which mobile devices to target.

⑥ References

Apple. 2010. "iPhone Technical Specifications." http://support.apple.com/kb/SP2.

Apple. 2014. "iPhone 6." https://www.apple.com/iphone-6/specs/.

Bixby, J. 2011. "Mobile Web User Expectations: 2009 vs. 2011." *Web Performance Today*, July 20. http://www.webperformancetoday.com/2011/07/20/new-findings-mobile-web-users-are-more-disappointed-than-ever/.

Chan, J. 2009. "HTC Dream." *CNET*, February 23. http://asia.cnet.com/product/htc-dream-44217759.htm.

Hooksett Public Library. 2014. "eReaders for Loan at Your Library." http://www.hooksettlibrary.org/reading/ereaders-for-loan-at-your-library/.

Kim, B. 2013. "The Present and Future of the Library Mobile Experience." *Library Technology Reports* 49, no. 6 (August/September): 15–28.

Samsung. 2014. "Galaxy S5." http://www.samsung.com/global/microsite/galaxys5/specs.html.

Sterling, G. 2013. "Users Prefer Apps to Mobile Sites but High Expectations Burn Developers." Internet 2GO, March 14. http://internet2go.net/news/data-and-forecasts/users -prefer-apps-mobile-sites-high-expectations-burn-developers.

CHAPTER 3

Deciding on and Planning Mobile Library Services and Resources

WITH THE GROWTH AND EXPANSION of mobile technology, and the increasing expectations of users, libraries and librarians are faced with the challenge, and opportunity, of disseminating information to users in this popular format. However, with the different types of mobile technology available, and the cost associated with the technology, it can be hard for librarians to determine just what types of mobile services and resources to offer. Librarians may struggle with which devices or mobile platforms to target. Additionally, librarians may wonder what types of mobile services to offer, as well as how to fund any endeavor into mobile technology. Depending on the route taken, the strategy and planning will vary. Regardless of the challenges associated with offering mobile services and resources to patrons, many libraries are seizing the opportunity and making mobile a priority. The first step for you and your library on the road to offering mobile services and resources is to determine what devices and mobile platforms you want to target.

⌾ Deciding What Mobile Technology to Target

With the various forms of mobile technology available, deciding which mobile services and resources to offer can seem like a daunting task. There are overall trends in mobile technology, but how do those trends reflect the mobile usage and behavior of your users? How can you tell? Are there certain types of mobile technology your library should be targeting to reach your mobile users? These are all questions, along with many others, that you and your library may be thinking about. There are several ways that you can evaluate and determine what mobile services and resources your library should offer and what mobile technology you should be targeting. One way is to research and examine the overall trends in mobile technology and the impact those technologies are having on the general public. This will give you an idea of the broad usage behaviors of the mobile user. While it may not be applicable to your library currently, it may give you an idea of what to expect in the not-so-distant future. Another aid for determining the mobile projects and initiatives your library may undertake is to gather statistical data from your users on what types of mobile technology they use. This can be done through surveys or statistics from your information technology department (if such IT stats are available). This allows you to get direct feedback from potential mobile users that will aid in the decision-making process. It also alerts your users that the library is aware of mobile technology and its role in society.

Pew Research Center

One place to start for identifying the overall trends in mobile technology is the Pew Research Center's Internet and American Life Project. According to their website, the Pew Research Center is a nonpartisan fact tank that informs the public about the issues, attitudes, and trends that are shaping global society. They conduct public-opinion polling, demographic research, media content analysis, and other empirical social science research (Pew Internet and American Life Project 2014a). Some of that research has focused solely on mobile technology. The Pew Research Center tracks statistics on the percentage of American adults that own a mobile phone, smartphone, e-reader, or tablet, as well as other usage behavior related to mobile technology. In April 2012, the Pew Research Center's Internet and American Life Project found that:

- 88 percent of American adults own a mobile phone.
- 46 percent of American adults own a smartphone.
- 18 percent of American adults own an e-reader.
- 18 percent of American adults own a tablet computer. (Pew Internet and American Life Project 2014b)

Comparatively, according to their January 2014 Mobile Technology Fact Sheet, they found that:

- 90 percent of American adults own a mobile phone.
- 58 percent of American adults own a smartphone.
- 32 percent of American adults own an e-reader.
- 42 percent of American adults own a tablet computer. (Pew Internet and American Life Project 2014c)

From these statistics, you can see that the adoption of mobile devices has increased rapidly over the last few years. This is a trend that will continue.

In addition to the overall statistics on mobile device ownership, the Pew Research Center tracks mobile usage behavior and breaks down mobile device ownership demographically. On mobile usage behavior, they found that:

- 67 percent of mobile phone owners found themselves checking their phones for messages, alerts, or calls even when they do not notice their mobile device ringing or vibrating.
- 49 percent of mobile phone owners have slept with their mobile phone next to their bed because they did not want to miss any calls, text messages, or other updates during the night.
- 29 percent of mobile phone owners describe their mobile phone as "something they can't imagine living without." (Pew Internet and American Life Project 2014c)

Libraries might also be interested in the demographic breakdown of smartphone ownership to help determine mobile services and resources to target specific mobile users. An example of a demographic breakdown provided by the Pew Research Center would be smartphone ownership across different age groups. They found that smartphone ownership breaks down as follows:

- Eighteen- to twenty-nine-year-olds, 83 percent own smartphones
- Thirty- to forty-nine-year-olds, 74 percent own smartphones
- Fifty- to sixty-four-year-olds, 49 percent own smartphones
- Sixty-five-year-olds and up, 19 percent own smartphones (Pew Internet and American Life Project 2014c)

The Pew Research Center also provides demographic information on smartphone ownership based on sex, race/ethnicity, education level, household income, and community type. Additionally, they track how individuals use their mobile devices. They even do research on e-readers, tablets, and libraries in the digital age. This research is aimed specifically at public libraries. The Pew Research Center provides a wealth of statistical information related to mobile technology that is valuable for libraries, as well as an overall view of the mobile landscape among adults in society.

Horizon Report

Another report on mobile technology that is relevant to libraries, more specifically academic and school libraries, is the Horizon Report. The Horizon Report is a project of the New Media Consortium in cooperation with the EDUCAUSE Learning Initiative. The project charts the landscape of emerging technologies for teaching, learning, and creative inquiry around the world. Since the inception of the project in 2002, the New Media Consortium has held ongoing conversations with technology professionals, campus technologists, faculty leaders from colleges and universities, and representatives of leading corporations (New Media Consortium 2014). The report is available in a few different editions that are of interest to academic and school libraries. Academic libraries will be interested in the Higher Education edition, and school libraries in the K-12 edition.

The 2012 Higher Education and K-12 editions of the Horizon Report identified mobile apps and tablets as emerging technology on the near-term horizon, meaning that they are expected to be adopted within one year. The 2012 K-12 edition also listed mobile devices as technology on the near-term horizon. The Higher Education edition found that mobile applications were the fastest growing dimension of the mobile landscape within higher education, and they impact nearly every academic discipline. The report also found that higher education institutions were designing applications tailored to educational and research needs across the curriculum (New Media Consortium 2012a).

The Horizon Report stated that the expansion of mobile devices and development of mobile applications have shifted the perception of software. With the development of these smaller pieces of software, users are able to outfit their mobile devices with the features available in some desktop software programs for a fraction of the cost. The report goes on to state that as higher education institutions begin to fully understand the potential of mobile applications, they are building in features that enable students to check grades, access the campus directory, update users with sports scores or campus news, and provide access to library resources (New Media Consortium 2012a). The increasing availability of network access means that the capabilities of mobile devices are available to more students in more locations each year. Higher education institutions are also investing in infrastructure that support mobile access, sponsoring programs that provide devices to students who do not already have them, and commissioning custom mobile applications to serve their communities (New Media Consortium 2012a). Judging from these developments, it is easy to see that mobile technology is playing a key role in higher education.

Another emerging technology identified in the 2012 Higher Education edition of the Horizon Report was tablet computing. The report identified tablet computing as a technology that presents new opportunities to enhance learning experiences that are not possible with other devices. Tablets were also seen as a supplement to smartphones since many consumers are using them in tandem with those mobile devices. Due to the larger display of tablets, and their ability to bring many of the same mobile apps available on smaller devices to that bigger display, higher education institutions are seeing them as an affordable solution for one-to-one learning. Additionally, tablets are seen as feature-rich tools for field and lab work that can often replace more expensive and cumbersome devices and equipment (New Media Consortium 2012a). The fact that students are familiar with these devices, as well as the expanding features available on the latest tablet models, has given higher education institutions incentives to integrate these devices into the curriculum.

Mobile devices and apps, as well as tablet computing, were also relevant technologies identified in the 2012 K-12 edition of the Horizon Report. Previously banned from classrooms, these technologies and devices have become such instrumental tools that schools are beginning to rethink their policies, with some even implementing "bring your own device" (BYOD) programs (New Media Consortium 2012b). The report goes on to state that as features continue to expand on mobile devices, they grow more and more interesting. In 2012, the report found that 61 percent of Americans aged twelve and older owned a mobile device, and 44 percent owned a smartphone (New Media Consortium 2012b). Taken in tandem with the statistics from the Pew Research Center, which examines mobile device ownership of those eighteen and older, these are telling statistics that shows the importance of mobile technology in society. Additionally, Common Sense Media found in 2013 that the percentage of children with access to some sort of smart mobile device at home jumped from 52 to 75 percent in two years (Common Sense Media 2013). Like higher education institutions, K-12 schools are seeing the benefits of mobile devices and apps and are looking at ways to integrate them into the curriculum. They are also investing resources in infrastructure to support mobile devices.

Tablets are another mobile technology identified in the Horizon Report as on the near horizon. Offering many of the same benefits to K-12 schools as they do to higher education institutions, tablets are becoming more integrated into curriculums. The report states that "the device [tablet] itself encourages exploration of it capabilities, something easily demonstrated by simply placing the device into the hands of a small child" (New Media Consortium 2012b). Because tablets are also designed to share screens easily, they foster twenty-first-century skills in students that include creativity, innovation, communication, and collaboration (New Media Consortium 2012b). As a result, more and more schools are turning to tablets as an ideal option for one-to-one learning deployment.

While these statistics and reports are not specific to libraries, they contain relevant information about the mobile usage behavior of potential users. They also signify the importance of mobile technology in society. Libraries can draw on this information to understand the types of mobile technology that students as well as the general public are using. It could be valuable in deciding what types of mobile services and resources to offer.

Surveys

Surveys are a way that you can elicit feedback from your specific users. They enable you to gain a more localized understanding of the mobile usage behaviors of your users, which can aid you and your library in determining the types of mobile services and resources to offer. Surveys also allow you to see the types of mobile services and resources your users may be interested in but don't yet own, which can be a key component in the decision-making process of what services to offer and support. At the Ensor Learning Resource Center at Georgetown College, a biennial survey is used to get feedback from users related to mobile devices and e-books. While the biennial survey is designed to provide feedback about overall satisfaction with the various services offered by the library, there are always some questions that aim to target topics relevant to users. In 2012, that topic was mobile technology and e-books.

Looking to delve more into mobile technology, the Ensor Learning Resource Center saw the survey as an opportunity to find out what types of mobile services and resources users were interested in and to determine what types of mobile projects the library should undertake. The 2012 survey included five prompts related to mobile technology and e-books:

- E-book reader preference
- Do you currently use a dedicated e-book reader or e-reader app?
- (For those who use one) what type of e-book reader or e-reader app do you use?
- Do you use a mobile device (i.e., iPod, Blackberry, cell phone, Android, tablet computer, iPad, etc.)?
- What mobile device(s) do you use? (Check all that apply)

A similar survey was undertaken by Hunter College Library. They created a library mobile technology survey to see how their students were using their mobile devices. They wanted to use the results to build a user-centered library website. The objectives of their mobile technology survey were:

- To gather data on the types of mobile devices students use
- To determine if students are using mobile devices for research purposes
- To discover what content students want offered on a mobile library website
- To create a user-center design for the mobile library website (Becker, Bonadie-Joseph, and Cain 2013)

Their survey included a list of thirty-three questions on the different devices that students interact with and what types of library services they access from their mobile devices.

An additional way to gather statistical data about the mobile devices your users are interacting with is by contacting your information technology (IT) department or the entity that oversees your network. Some IT departments keep track of the types of devices that access the local network. They are able to track the usage of mobile devices and mobile operating systems when users log on or access the wireless network. The IT department at Georgetown College keeps track of these statistics and even breaks them down to show the mobile devices and mobile operating systems that faculty and staff use to access the wireless network. These statistics do not include users that do not connect to the wireless network to access the Internet and other resources. The Ensor Learning Resource Center staff requested these statistics from the IT department to see the types of mobile devices and mobile operating systems that were prevalent among the campus community; the statistics in table 3.1 are from January 1, 2014, to May 15, 2014.

Focus Groups

Focus groups can be used to get feedback from your users about the types of mobile devices they use, as well as the types of mobile services and resources they would like to see offered at your library. When setting up a focus group, you will want to establish what the main objectives are, how many users there will be, the duration, and the role you may have as the moderator or note taker. North Carolina State University Libraries is an example of a library that has used focus groups (North Carolina State University Libraries 2014).

Using all of these methods, as well as others you may find applicable, will give you and your library an understanding of the overall trends in mobile technology. It also gives

Table 3.1. Top Mobile Operating Systems, Georgetown College

	OPERATING SYSTEM	# CLIENTS	% CLIENTS	USAGE
1	Apple iOS	3197	79.9%	22.79 TB
2	Android	620	15.5%	2.33 TB
3	Generic Android	185	4.6%	81.82 GB

you a localized understanding of how mobile technology is impacting your users. With the data gathered, you can decide what types of mobile services and resources to offer and move on to planning and developing them.

⑥ Planning

At this point, you have examined the overall trends in mobile technology and evaluated feedback from your users. Regardless of what types of mobile services and resources you decide to offer, in order for them to be successful, you will need to plan properly. An essential part of planning is to identify your goals. For example, goals that your library may have in mind could include:

- Enhancing the convenience of access to reference services
- Enhancing the convenience of access to basic library and patron information
- Encouraging individuals who generally do not use the library's services to access the library
- Supporting a campuswide or departmental initiative employing mobile devices
- Enhancing the library's instruction program, both in the classroom and beyond
- Providing e-books and e-readers to users as an alternative to some print publications
- Delivering easy-to-access, key information resources to users in the field
- Providing campus-related, geographically linked content to enrich the campus experience of users
- Becoming a campus resource for educating users about the features and operation of mobile devices
- Raising the profile of the library, its staff, and its services (Lippencott 2010)

Your goals may differ depending on what types of services and resources your library decides to offer. There are some broad questions that you may need to consider:

- What is the current state of mobile device deployment at your institution or for your population?
- What are your goals for providing service, and what are your strategies?
- Who should you work with within your institution or service area?
- How will you know if you are successful?
- What is your strategy for the next two or three years? (Lippencott 2010)

You and your library will need to consider these broad questions, along with others, as you determine your strategy for mobile services. Once you have a specific service or resource that you are going to be initiating, through either a vendor or internal development, additional issues will arise that you will need to address. For example, if you are implementing a text reference service, you may consider the following questions:

- What are the costs associated with different service delivery models?
- What is financially feasible in the short term and the long term?
- Should text reference service be integrated with existing virtual reference services?
- How much extra work is reasonable for librarians in adapting to the new service?
- What is the acceptable amount of instruction to users?

- What features of the software are important?
- What built-in tools of the service are essential? (Luo 2013)

These are just a sample of some of the questions that you may consider when you decide what type of mobile services to offer at your library.

If your library is planning to develop a mobile website, there are some different considerations since this initiative is more technical in nature. Bohyun Kim offers a list of tips for developing a mobile website for your library:

- Do an environmental scan to see what libraries have mobile websites, and what services and resources they are offering.
- Identify what your library's capabilities are in regard to building a mobile website.
- Find out what types of mobile devices your users own, and what they expect when they visit a mobile website.
- Pick only services and resources that are useful on a mobile device.
- Make the scope of your project explicit.
- Take advantage of existing mobile frameworks like jQuery Mobile.
- Define roles for your team members involved in the development.
- Let your users test it before it is officially launched.
- Make sure to track the usage by adding Google Analytics or a similar service. (Kim 2012)

These are some of the considerations that go into planning the development of a mobile website for your library. These can also be applied if you are exploring the possibility of developing a native application.

If your library is exploring the possibility of lending mobile devices, you will need to determine what types of devices to lend. Will your library be lending tablets, e-readers, or a combination of the two? With so many mobile devices on the market, it can be a difficult choice. If you are trying to decide what mobile devices would be beneficial for your users, it might be helpful to list the advantages and disadvantages of the devices your library is considering. For example, a list of advantages for the Amazon Kindle might include:

- Easy to operate
- Easy to purchase
- Easy to download Kindle e-books with Wi-Fi or 3G connection
- Lots of free Kindle e-books
- Can download content to six devices (Bischoff, Rawlins, and Ruth 2013)

And a list of disadvantages for the Amazon Kindle might include:

- Amazon's one-click payment can be a challenge for libraries
- Can only purchase one title at a time
- Deregistering Kindles before circulation so users cannot purchase content
- Tax (must have tax-exempt certificate on file with Amazon for Amazon Digital Services)

- E-books sold by sellers other than Amazon will accrue tax, and each seller has to be contacted individually for a tax refund (Bischoff, Rawlins, and Ruth 2013)

Developing these lists can help you determine what mobile devices are the best fit for your library and users. These are examples of what your library will need to evaluate when planning to offer mobile services and resources. However, the considerations and factors will vary from library to library.

Funding

An important variable in mobile projects is funding. Whether you are offering a mobile-optimized service like text reference or lending mobile devices, funding needs to be secured in order to provide mobile services and resources. Depending on the organizational structure of your library, you may need the approval of the library director or the governing authority (i.e., provost or board of trustees) before you can initiate a mobile project, even if the budget is available. Gaining approval may involve submitting a proposal outlining the benefits of the mobile project as well as the cost associated with a mobile initiative of this nature. If the funds are not available in your budget or the purchase may cause an unnecessary burden, you may need to seek funding through an external source such as a grant or through special one-time funding from your institution. This involves identifying the types of grants available and submitting an application for funding, or preparing a special funds request based on institutional guidelines. L. E. Phillips Memorial Public Library in Wisconsin is an example of a library able to provide access to mobile devices through an external funding source. Through a contribution from the Presto Foundation, they were able to purchase iPads to lend to their users.

Policies and Procedures

Once funding has been secured, your library will need to establish policies and procedures governing the use of your mobile services. For example, you will need to establish the policies and procedures for lending mobile devices. These will vary for each individual library. Some of the main considerations and questions that will need to be addressed for lending mobile devices include:

- Length of time the device can be checked out
- Can the device be renewed?
- Does the device have to remain in the library or can users take it out of the library?
- Late fines and fees
- Replacement costs
- Can users load their own content?
- Do users need to sign a loan agreement once or every time the device is checked out?

The answer to these questions will vary depending on what your library feels is appropriate and reasonable. Additionally, you will need to develop policies and procedures for maintaining and updating the devices once your users return them. This involves charging, loading new content, and many other considerations. Once you have reached this point, you are ready to initiate and develop mobile services for your library.

◎ Key Points

A lot goes into to deciding what mobile services and resources you will offer at your library. Important aspects include evaluating the overall trends in mobile technology, feedback from your users, and planning the services and resources.

- According to statistics and reports from the Pew Research Center and the New Media Consortium, mobile technology is expanding in society and becoming an integral part of education.
- Surveys are a good way for libraries to gather feedback directly from users.
- Planning mobile services and resources involves setting goals, securing funding for the project, and developing policies and procedures to govern your mobile services.

Now that you have decided what mobile technology to target, you are ready to begin developing the services and resources. The next chapter will cover how libraries can develop mobile websites.

◎ References

Bischoff, Helen, Ben Rawlins, and Michele Ruth. 2013. "Making the Library Mobile on a Shoestring Budget." In *Mobile Library Services: Best Practices*, edited by Charles Harmon and Michael Messina, 43–54. Lanham, MD: Scarecrow Press.

Becker, Danielle, Ingrid Bonadie-Jospeh, and Jonathan Cain. 2013. "Developing and Completing a Library Mobile Technology Survey to Create a User-Centered Mobile Presence." *Library Hi Tech* 31, no. 4 (November): 688–99.

Common Sense Media. 2013. "New Research from Common Sense Media Reveals Mobile Media Use among Young Children Has Tripled in Two Years." October 28. http://www.common sensemedia.org/about-us/news/press-releases/new-research-from-common-sense-media -reveals-mobile-media-use-among.

Kim, B. 2012. "Twenty Tips for Creating Your Library's First Mobile Web Site." *Reference Librarian* 53, no. 3 (July): 310–12.

Lippencott, J. 2010. "Mobile Reference: What Are the Questions?" *Reference Librarian* 51, no. 1 (January/March): 1–11.

Luo, Lili. 2013. "Text a Librarian: Ideas for Best Practices." In *The Handheld Library: Mobile Technology and the Librarian*, edited by Thomas A. Peters and Lori Bell, 43–54. Santa Barbara, CA: Libraries Unlimited.

New Media Consortium. 2012a. "NMC Horizon Report > 2012 Higher Education Edition." http://www.nmc.org/pdf/2012-horizon-report-HE.pdf.

———. 2012b. "NMC Horizon Report > 2012 K-12 Edition." http://www.nmc.org/pdf/2012 -horizon-report-K12.pdf.

———. 2014. "About the NMC Horizon Report > 2014 Higher Education Edition." http:// horizon.wiki.nmc.org/About.

North Carolina State University Libraries. 2014. "User Studies." http://www.lib.ncsu.edu/user studies.

Pew Internet and American Life Project. 2014a. "About the Project." http://www.pewinternet .org/about/.

———. 2014b. "Device Ownership over Time." http://www.pewinternet.org/data-trend/mobile/ device-ownership/.

———. 2014c. "Mobile Technology Fact Sheet." http://www.pewinternet.org/fact-sheets/mobile -technology-fact-sheet/.

CHAPTER 4

Developing Mobile-Optimized Library Websites

IN THIS CHAPTER
▷ Understanding the advantages and disadvantages of mobile websites
▷ Using mobile frameworks to develop mobile library websites
▷ Developing a mobile library website with the jQuery Mobile framework
▷ Developing a library website with responsive Web design

A S MOBILE WEB TRAFFIC CONTINUES TO INCREASE and mobile devices become more robust, users expect to be able to consume information in a mobile-friendly manner. With the wealth of information that users have access to through libraries, it stands to reason that libraries must strive to make their resources accessible in a mobile format. One way that libraries and other organizations are doing that is through the development of mobile websites. With the variety of different frameworks and tools available for developers, providing content and information in a mobile format is easier than ever and essential to meet the needs of library users.

Mobile Library Websites

There are a variety of different design and development options available to libraries looking to provide mobile-optimized access to library resources and services. Those options include developing a separate mobile website, using responsive Web design to develop library websites, and developing native applications to target specific mobile platforms (this option will be discussed in later chapters). For now, let's look at the advantages and disadvantages of creating a mobile website, as well as the tools and frameworks available to do so.

Mobile websites are scaled-down versions of larger websites that are designed and optimized for viewing on mobile devices. They may even be hosted on their own sub-domain, such as m.yourlibrary.com. The general purpose of a mobile website is to make the content, or at least a subset of the content, available to your users. Mobile websites complement the existing library website and help extend resources and information to users through their mobile devices. As with any project, there are distinct advantages and disadvantages to developing a separate mobile library website.

Advantages

One advantage of developing a mobile library website is that it only needs to be developed once, unlike native applications that need to be developed for each specific mobile platform. In essence, this means mobile websites are device agnostic since they will work across a variety of different mobile platforms such as iOS, Android, and Windows Mobile. With a mobile website, users get the same experience interacting with the mobile website regardless of what mobile device they are using. Users will just need to visit a Web address instead of downloading an additional piece of software through an app store. Users with feature phones may also be able to access the mobile library website.

Another advantage of mobile websites is that they are easier to maintain than native applications. Since the content is maintained on a Web server, changes can be made relatively quickly and in real time. With native applications, any changes that are made have to go through the mobile platform's app store and are often not available immediately after submission. Additionally, changes made to native applications require users to download those updates, which can often lead to users not having the most current version of the application on their device. With a mobile website, users do not need to download an update. The library makes any needed changes to the site, and the user benefits immediately.

A third advantage of developing a mobile library website is that it is more cost effective than developing a native application. Developing native apps for specific platforms requires the payment of developer fees. These can be a one-time fee or a yearly fee. On the other hand, the development of a mobile website does not require the payment of any developer fees. All that is needed is an understanding of HTML and CSS (although skills in HTML5 and PHP can be useful for creating more engaging websites), as well as access to a Web server.

Additional advantages of mobile websites are that they are easier to find and have a broader reach than native applications. Users can find mobile websites through search engine results and links on the library's website. Mobile websites also have a bigger audience than native applications. Mobile websites are device agnostic; they can reach users on any mobile platform since all that is required is a Web browser. You can probably think of other advantages of developing a mobile website for your library.

Disadvantages

Despite the many advantages of developing a mobile library website, there are some disadvantages as well. For example, mobile websites require access to the Internet, which could result in slower load and response times if there is not a good Wi-Fi or cellular network connection, creating a poor experience for users, whereas native applications are installed on the device (locally) and do not require an Internet connection, resulting in better performance than mobile websites.

Another disadvantage of mobile websites is that they are currently not able to access some of the specific features of a mobile device that a native application can. For example, mobile websites cannot access the camera functionality of a mobile device. However, there are strides being made in HTML5 that are looking to minimize this.

A third disadvantage of a mobile website is that it is an additional website that needs to be maintained. While a mobile website needs to be developed once and is accessible on different mobile platforms, it still needs to be updated when the library's regular website is updated to reflect current information. These are some of the main disadvantages of developing mobile library websites. Despite the disadvantages, many organizations, libraries included, are developing mobile websites to reach users with mobile devices.

⑥ Mobile Frameworks

There are a variety of different frameworks that librarians can use to develop mobile websites. While mobile websites can be created by manually coding and creating the site in HTML and CSS, mobile frameworks can help to make the creation of a mobile website easier. Many mobile frameworks are available as paid options; however, a good selection of mobile frameworks are freely available. Examples of freely available mobile frameworks include iWebKit, jQT (formerly jQTouch), Sencha Touch, and jQuery Mobile.

The iWebKit mobile framework is a file package that enables librarians and other developers to create mobile websites that are compatible with various iOS mobile devices. Although the look of the related website with this framework closely resembles navigation that many iOS users are familiar with, it is compatible with a majority of devices. The framework is easy to understand and does not required advanced knowledge of HTML.

Another freely available mobile framework is jQT. This framework is a Zepto/jQuery plugin for mobile Web development that supports a wide variety of mobile platforms and devices. It is optimized for WebKit browsers, which is an open source Web browser engine. The jQT framework is designed to give the mobile website the look and feel of a native application. It works as one big HTML file. Once jQT is downloaded, you will need to create a <div> tag inside the <body> tag for each section or page of the mobile website. You will need to use class naming conventions in HTML for stylistic purposes (div.toolbar, ul.rounded, etc.), and then add the appropriate Java-Script (jqtouch.min.js and jqtouch-jquery.js) and CSS (jqtouch.css and theme.css) files inside the <head> tag. Additionally, a call for the jQTouch function, .jQTouch(), will need to be added inside the <head> tag as well. Features of this mobile framework include native WebKit animations, callback events, themes, swipe detection, and additional extensions. It is now part of Sencha Labs, which is where the next mobile framework comes from as well.

Sencha Touch is an HTML5 mobile framework that is compatible with the major mobile platforms. It comes with fifty built-in components and themes for the different mobile platforms. This framework also has a built-in model-view-controller (MVC) system, which is a software pattern for implementing user interfaces. Some features of Sencha Touch include animations, DOM manipulations, AJAX, and touch events. It is licensed under free commercial and open source licenses for application development, as well as a paid commercial license for OEM uses.

One of the more popular mobile frameworks is jQuery Mobile. The jQuery Mobile framework is a touch-optimized HTML5 framework that is accessible across a majority of mobile platforms. Some of the key features of this framework include support for touch and mouse events, working with assistive technologies such as screen readers, AJAX-powered navigation, theming framework, animated page transitions, UI widgets, and a host of other options. In addition to these features, jQuery Mobile enables developers to create custom themes through the use of the ThemeRoller tool.

The jQuery Mobile framework is a popular choice for libraries as well. North Carolina State University Libraries uses jQuery Mobile for a variety of their mobile projects, such as their photographic and historic campus tour, WolfWalk. Other libraries that use jQuery Mobile for their mobile website include Montana State University Libraries, the Free Library of Philadelphia, Boise Public Library, Chesapeake College Learning Resource Center, and a host of others. OCLC also uses this framework for the mobile versions of individual WorldCat library websites. For example, Georgetown College's Ensor Learning Resource Center's WorldCat mobile website uses jQuery Mobile (http://georgetowncollege.worldcat.org/m/). For libraries that use the Ex Libris ILS Voyager, there are mobile resources developed by other librarians that use jQuery Mobile. For example, the Voyager shelf list program ShelfLister 3.0, developed by the University of Texas at Arlington's system librarian, Michael Doran, uses jQuery Mobile. Additionally, Denise Dunham from the University of Rochester developed a mobile skin for the Voyager online catalog using jQuery Mobile. Since this is a popular framework for libraries, let's take a closer look at the structure of a jQuery Mobile website and how to use it to build a mobile library website.

Building a Mobile Library Website with jQuery Mobile

One reason that jQuery Mobile may be popular among libraries and other developers is that it is not a difficult framework to understand. There are a lot of documented examples with the source code available on the jQuery Mobile website. It is similar to the jQT framework in that the entire website can consist of only one HTML file. It is not limited to that, however, since a separate HTML file can be created for each page within the website. For the example that will be provided here, the approach is to create just one file. But first, let's look at the structure of a jQuery Mobile website. The code for a basic one-page website would be similar to the following example:

```
<!DOCTYPE html>
<html>
<head>
<title>Mobile Library Website</title>
<meta name="viewport" content="width=device-width, initial-scale=1">
<link rel="stylesheet" href="http://code.jquery.com/mobile/1.4.2/jquery.mobile-1.4.2.min.css">
<script src="http://code.jquery.com/jquery-1.10.2.min.js"></script>
```

```
<script src="http://code.jquery.com/mobile/1.4.1/jquery
.mobile-1.4.2.min.js"></script>
</head>
<body>

<div data-role="page">
<div data-role="header">
<h1>Mobile Library Website</h1>
</div>

<div data-role="main" class="ui-content">
<!--Page Content Goes Here-->
</div>

<div data-role="footer">
<h1>Footer Text</h1>
</div>
</div>

</body>
</html>
```

Each section of the markup tells the developer what the specific function is of the particular <div>. The <div data-role="page"> is the page that is displayed within a Web browser. The <div data-role="header"> creates a toolbar at the top of the page that is used for titles and/or navigation buttons. The <div data-role="main"> defines the main content of the page where the text, images, buttons, or other content will go, and the "ui-content" class adds extra padding and margin inside the page content. Like the <div data-role="header">, the <div data-role="footer"> creates a toolbar, but it is located at the bottom of the page. Inside these containers you can customize and add HTML elements to suit the needs of your library. Adding additional pages to a jQuery Mobile website is not difficult; you will just need to add the following and then customize each page.

```
<div data-role="page">
<div data-role="header">
<h1>Mobile Library Website</h1>
</div>

<div data-role="main" class="ui-content">
<!--Page Content Goes Here-->
</div>

<div data-role="footer">
<h1>Footer Text</h1>
</div>
</div>
```

Now that you have an idea of what the basic structure of a jQuery Mobile website looks like, it is time to start creating a mobile website for your library using this framework. At this point, you have decided what elements you want to include in the mobile website.

The Ensor Learning Resource Center (LRC) at Georgetown College decided to include the following elements in their jQuery Mobile library website:

- Hours
- Catalog Search
- Research
- Ask-a-Librarian
- Directory
- My Account
- Library Maps

Additionally, the library added a navigation bar above the footer to include a link to the full library website as well as a link to the native applications the library created. These are the resources and services that were seen as essential to have in the mobile website. These may be the same elements that your library chooses to include, or you may select some variation. Here is a breakdown of how the Ensor Learning Resource Center used the jQuery Mobile framework to build the home page of the library's mobile website. For the header portion, there were some additional CSS elements added to customize the header for the logo. Here is the coding for the header portion of the library's mobile website:

```
<div data-role="header" data-theme="d">
<div class="banner" align="center"><img src="http://www
.georgetowncollege.edu/wp-content/themes/library-arras/
images/lrc-logo.png" title="Ensor LRC" alt="Ensor LRC
Logo"/>
</div>
</div>
```

The following CSS element was added to set a max width for the logo across a variety of different devices.

```
img.banner {
width: 100%;
max-width: 600px;
}
```

The primary content of the main page is encased within a listview. There are a few different listview options in jQuery Mobile, and the Ensor Learning Resource Center chose to display the home page content in a linked listview that spans the width of the page.

```
<div data-role="main">
<ul data-role="listview" data-theme="d">
<li><a href="#hours">Hours</a></li>
<li><a href="#catalog" data-rel="dialog">Catalog Search
</a></li>
<li><a href="#mobile">Research</a></li>
<li><a href="#ask">Ask-A-Librarian</a></li>
```

```
<li><a href="#directory">Directory</a></li>
<li><a href="https://voyager.georgetowncollege.edu/vwebv/
login?sk=mobile"
rel="external">My Account</a></li>
<li><a href="#maps">Library Maps</a></li>
</ul>
</div>
```

The "ui-content" class was removed since there was no need for the extra padding or margin. Thus links to other pages in the list are contained in the same HTML file, except for the My Account option, which links out to an external Web page. Links to external pages will be loaded via Ajax; however, if the Ajax request fails, you will receive the "Error Loading Page" message. To avoid this, you can add rel="external" after the link to open the external page without Ajax.

The last part of the home page is the footer section. For this section, some additional jQuery Mobile elements were added, such as the navigation bar that rests right above the footer logo. The navigation bar contains three "bars" or links: a link to a mobile website developed and released as open source by Jason Clark of Montana State University called BookMeUp, a link to the library's full website, and a link to a page within the mobile website to download the applications created by the library for iOS and Android. Here is the markup for the footer section:

```
<div data-role="footer" data-theme="d">
<div data-role="navbar">
<ul>
<li><a href="http://www.georgetowncollege.edu/wp-content/
themes/library-arras/bookme/index.php" data-theme="a"
rel="external">BookMeUp</a></li>
<li><a href="http://www.georgetowncollege.edu/library"
data-theme="a" rel="external">Full Site</a></li>
<li><a href="#lrcapp" data-rel="dialog" data-theme="a">LRC
Apps</a></li>
</ul>
</div>
<h1><a href="http://www.georgetowncollege.edu/"><img
src="http://www.georgetowncollege.edu/wp-content/themes/
library-arras/mobile/images/livelearn.gif" /></a></h1>
</div>
```

These are the elements that make up the home page of the Ensor Learning Resource Center's jQuery Mobile website. If you are using these elements as an example, make sure that you include <div data-role="page"> before the header and add an additional <div> tag after the footer to complete the page. The result of this markup is seen in figure 4.1.

The jQuery Mobile framework has a good set of demos that lets developers see and interact with the different elements included in the framework. Want to see how to create a listview in jQuery Mobile? They have examples and provide you with source code for each example, which makes it easy to implement into your mobile library website. You can also customize what elements of the framework you want to download using the

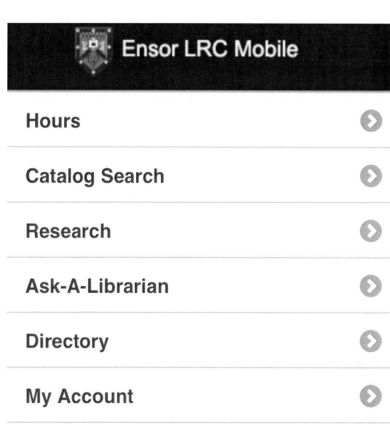

Figure 4.1. Ensor LRC Mobile website.

Download Builder feature. This framework can also be used in conjunction with a program called PhoneGap to build native applications (more on that later).

Using Content Management Systems to Create Mobile Library Websites

In addition to building a mobile website with jQuery Mobile or one of the other frameworks previously listed, there are ways to make your library website mobile if you are working within the confines of a content management system like WordPress. WordPress is an open source content management platform that many libraries are using to maintain their websites. This platform has a wide variety of website themes and plugins to extend the functionality of websites without having to build the website from the ground up. In addition to the various website themes, there are a variety of different plugins for WordPress that can help make your library website mobile without the need to do any additional coding.

Examples of freely available WordPress mobile plugins include WPTouch, Mobile Smart Pro, and WP Mobile Edition. A host of other options are also available, but some of those come with a high cost. Many of the mobile plugins just mentioned detect when a user is on a mobile device and automatically convert your library website into a mobile-friendly format. Using a mobile plugin is just one way that you can create a mobile library website in a content management system like WordPress.

Another way to create a mobile website in a content management system is by creating a mobile template and assigning that template to one of the pages in the website. For example, in WordPress, a simple way to create a template is to first add a small piece of PHP coding such as:

```
<?php
/*
 * Template Name: Mobile
 */
?>
```

After this is added, you can proceed to add the HTML markup for your mobile library website. For example, you could add the coding for the mobile library website you built using jQuery Mobile or another mobile framework. These are a few ways to create a mobile website within a content management system like WordPress. However, there is another way that is becoming more and more popular for building not only mobile websites, but full websites, and that is the use of responsive Web design.

Responsive Web Design

A second approach to creating a mobile-optimized library website is by using responsive Web design. Responsive Web design aims at providing an optimal Web page viewing experience across of broad range of devices from smartphones to desktop computers. The term was made popular by Ethan Marcotte, a Web designer and developer; he states that responsive Web design offers us a way forward, finally allowing us to "design for the ebb and flow of things" (Marcotte 2010). The popularity of this approach can be attributed to the increasing use of mobile devices.

Prior to the introduction of responsive Web design, many developers, libraries included, followed the principle of pixel-perfect Web design. Pixel-perfect Web design treats a Web page like a page from a magazine, and the mockup for the site is often done in a program like Photoshop. The goal of pixel-perfect Web design is to make the Web page look as much like the mockup as possible (Kim 2013). The issue with this approach is that Web pages designed this way are not scalable, meaning that when the browser window is resized, the Web page does not render well to smaller screen sizes. The pixel-perfect approach defines elements of the page to be specific widths in the CSS files. An example would be the CSS markup for a container on a Web page:

```
.container {
width:1024px;
}
```

Given that mobile devices come in a variety of different screen sizes, responsive Web design aims to solve some of the issues of pixel-perfect Web design with the use of three tools:

- Flexible, grid-based layout
- Flexible images
- Media queries

Flexible grids are created using relative units of measurements, like percentages, instead of absolute units of measurements, like pixels. The container markup from the previous example now becomes:

```
.container {
width:95%;
}
```

Additionally, CSS allows the library developer to make images more flexible by controlling them and other fixed-width elements to ensure that they remain in the container that they are assigned to. The media queries element of responsive Web design allows different CSS files to be applied depending on the media type and the maximum width of a device screen. Media queries will resemble the following:

```
@media screen and (min-width: 900px) {...}
@media screen and (max-width: 600px) {...}
@media screen and (max-width: 480px) {...}
```

Within the media queries, you would define the CSS element that would apply to devices with screen sizes that fit into the parameters of each media query. With responsive Web design, there is no longer one fixed layout for the library's website. Instead, the elements of the website are rearranged and adjusted according to the screen size of the device a user is accessing the library website with.

Advantages of Responsive Web Design

There are some distinct advantages to creating a library website using responsive Web design from both the library developer's perspective and the perspective of the user. For the library developer, a responsive website eliminates the need to have a separate mobile website. This means that there is only one website to maintain. It also means that the link for the library's website will be the same regardless of the device that is being used. Another advantage for the library developer is that although responsive websites are not automatically accessible, it is simpler for library developers to create a single markup of a site that meets accessibility guidelines, which can then scale appropriately to other contexts (Rempel and Bridges 2013).

From the user's perspective, a responsive website presents the same information that is available on the full library website. A responsive website is also easier for users to navigate since the elements are formatted based on screen size. Additionally, it provides users with a familiar interface and experience across a range of devices with which they may access the library's website.

Disadvantages of Responsive Web Design

Despite the advantages for both the library developer and the user, there are some disadvantages to responsive Web design. One disadvantage of responsive Web design is users are confined to the interface that the website renders based on the device they are using. The performance of responsive websites can be an issue as load times can often be longer than that of a mobile website. The speed of your library website could load slower depending on how many images have to be re-rendered for your responsive website. Another potential issue, albeit one that the library has little control over, is linking out to resources that are not optimized for mobile devices.

Libraries using responsive Web design include the University of North Carolina at Chapel Hill, Michigan State University Libraries, and Canton Public Library, among others. There are several reasons that libraries are moving, or looking to move, to a responsive website. Chief among them is that mobile users are accessing the full library website from mobile devices and bypassing the library's mobile website, as shown by statistics from the Ensor Learning Resource Center. Statistics from August 1, 2012 (when a new website and mobile website were launched), through December 31, 2013, show that there were 305 visits to the library's mobile website using mobile devices. During that same time period, there were 3,491 visits to the library's full website using mobile devices. That is ten times more visits to the library's full website using mobile devices than visits to the site specifically optimized for mobile devices. What this signifies is that mobile users want access to the same information available to them when using a desktop or laptop computer. It is possible that they do not want their options limited to what is offered on the mobile website. That is a major reason that the Ensor Learning Resource Center is now moving to a responsive website.

Creating a Responsive Website

If your library uses a content management system like WordPress or Drupal, a variety of tools are available to help you create a responsive website. If you are building a responsive website from scratch, there also are tools available to assist you, such as Bootstrap. Bootstrap is an open source collection of tools for creating websites and Web applications. It contains HTML and CSS-based design templates as well as optional JavaScript extensions. The starter template for a website built with Bootstrap is as follows:

```
<!DOCTYPE html>
<html lang="en">
<head>
<meta charset="utf-8">
<meta http-equiv="X-UA-Compatible" content="IE=edge">
<meta name="viewport" content="width=device-width,
initial-scale=1">
<title>Bootstrap 101 Template</title>

<!-- Bootstrap -->
<link href="css/bootstrap.min.css" rel="stylesheet">

<!-- HTML5 Shim and Respond.js IE8 support of HTML5 ele-
ments and media queries -->
```

```
<!-- WARNING: Respond.js doesn't work if you view the page
via file:// -->
<!--[if lt IE 9]>
<script src="https://oss.maxcdn.com/libs/html5shiv/3.7.0/
html5shiv.js"></script>
<script src="https://oss.maxcdn.com/libs/respond.js/1.4.2/
respond.min.js"></script>
<![endif]-->
</head>
<body>
<h1>Hello, world!</h1>

<!-- jQuery (necessary for Bootstrap's JavaScript plugins)
-->
<script src="https://ajax.googleapis.com/ajax/libs/
jquery/1.11.0/jquery.min.js"></script>
<!-- Include all compiled plugins (below), or include in-
dividual files as needed -->
<script src="js/bootstrap.min.js"></script>
</body>
</html>
```

Using the other elements and examples, you can build off of the basic template to create a responsive library website. The Bootstrap website provides examples and demos of the different elements that can be used to customize the basic template such as themes, grids, and navigation bars. The framework is supported by the latest versions of major Web browsers like Google Chrome and Firefox. This is just one tool that libraries can use to create a responsive website.

Another responsive framework is ZURB Foundation. Like Bootstrap, this framework is an open source collection of tools for creating websites and Web applications. It contains HTML and CSS-based design templates as well as optional JavaScript extensions. This framework comes packaged with a flexible grid layout, a prebuilt CSS file for all of the HTML elements, advanced components, and JavaScript plugins based on Zepto.js (a lighter alternative to jQuery). The ZURB Foundation framework is built with small mobile devices as a main priority and goes up from there. It is also built with Syntactically Awesome Stylesheets (Sass). Additionally, the framework is customizable.

Responsinator is a useful tool when developing a website using responsive Web design. This website allows you to enter the link for your library's website and see how it displays across a ranges of devices with different resolutions. However, it is still a good idea to test your responsive website on actual devices as well.

Developing a website using responsive Web design requires a different way of thinking. No longer are you, as the developer, creating a website just for a desktop, but you are creating a website that is scalable and optimized for a variety of different devices. Responsive Web design is often described as taking a mobile-first approach. In fact, it is Google's recommendation for building mobile websites. Their developer website states:

> Responsive design: serves the same HTML for one URL and uses CSS media queries
> to determine how the content is rendered on the client side. This removes the possible

glitches of user-agent detection and frees users from redirects. This is Google's recommended configuration. (Google Developers 2013)

Responsive Web design is becoming a more popular solution now as libraries, as well as other organizations, are transitioning or developing websites using this approach.

Regardless of whether you decide to build a separate mobile website or a responsive website, there are some factors that you need to keep in mind. According to Bohyun Kim, unnecessary content needs to be removed from the library website, especially the home page, so that users are able to locate the essential information and services they are looking for. Libraries need to keep uniformity of content across both the full website and the mobile website, as well as prioritize and organize the content differently on smaller screens so essential information is easy to locate and access (Kim 2013). These, as well as other considerations, are important factors when developing a website with your mobile users in mind.

Key Points

There are two ways that you can develop a mobile-optimized website: one is by using a mobile framework, such as jQuery Mobile; the other is using responsive Web design to develop your library's website.

- The jQuery Mobile framework is a valuable tool you can use to develop a mobile website for your library.
- Responsive Web design is becoming a popular option for library websites since there is only one code set that needs to be maintained and updated.
- If your library uses a content management system such as WordPress, you can create a mobile template or activate a mobile plugin to provide a mobile-optimized website.

Developing mobile library websites is just one way libraries can extend their resources and reach mobile users. Libraries are also targeting specific mobile platforms through the development of native applications. The next chapter will cover how libraries can develop native applications for the iOS platform.

References

Google Developers. 2013. "Building Smartphone-Optimized Websites." December 19. https:// developers.google.com/webmasters/smartphone-sites/.

Kim, B. 2013. "The Library Mobile Experience: Practices and User Expectations." *Library Technology Reports* 49, no. 6 (August/September): 29–39.

Marcotte, E. 2010. "Responsive Web Design." *A List Apart*, no. 391 (May 25). http://alistapart .com/article/responsive-web-design/.

Rempel, Hannah, and Laurie Bridges. 2013. "That Was Then, This Is Now: Replacing the Mobile-Optimized Site with Responsive Design." *Information Technology and Libraries* 32, no. 4 (November/December): 8–24.

CHAPTER 5

Developing Library Applications for iOS

CREATING NATIVE APPLICATIONS FOR ANY PLATFORM can seem like a daunting task. Each platform has a different programming language that needs to be learned. Despite these challenges, there are ways that librarians, as developers, can create native applications for iOS without having to learn a new programming language. Instead, library developers can use the PhoneGap framework to develop applications for iOS with existing Web technologies such as HTML, CSS, and JavaScript.

Native Applications

Along with developing mobile Web interfaces to reach mobile users, some libraries are focusing on developing native applications for specific mobile platforms such as Apple's iOS and Google's Android mobile operating systems. A native application is software that is designed to run on a device's specific mobile operating system. It is only compatible with that particular operating system. For example, a native application designed for iOS will not be operational on a device that runs Android, and vice versa. Native applications differ from mobile websites, also known as mobile Web apps, because they need to be developed for each operating system. Each mobile operating system has a different programming language, whereas mobile Web apps only need to be developed once and are compatible across a wide array of devices regardless of the mobile operating system. The primary programming language for iOS is Objective-C (although that will soon change with the introduction of Apple's new programming language, Swift), which is a general-purpose, object-oriented programming language. The primary programming language for Android is Java, which is a general-purpose, class-based, object-oriented programming language. There are a variety of other existing mobile platforms, such as Windows Mobile and Blackberry, but iOS and Android currently dominate the mobile platform market. Together, iOS and Android control around 90 percent of the market (IDC 2013). As a result many developers, libraries included, are focusing exclusively on these two mobile platforms.

While native applications need to be developed for each specific mobile platform, there are some significant advantages over mobile websites. Advantages of native applications include:

- A better user experience
- Faster than mobile websites
- Ability to use the application offline
- Integration of specific phone features such as GPS, camera functionality, and push notifications
- Easier to find in app stores such as Apple's App Store and the Google Play store

Additionally, mobile user behavior also factors into the decision of whether or not to develop native applications. The current trend is that mobile users are spending more time using native applications, which has led not only companies and corporations to develop native applications but libraries as well. The development of native applications enables libraries to target specific mobile platforms to connect users with library resources from the mobile platform of their choice. A search of Apple's App Store reveals that several libraries have developed applications for the iOS platform; examples include the District of Columbia Public Library, the Orange County Library System, and North Carolina State University Libraries.

The District of Columbia Public Library was the first public library to offer an iOS application. It was designed for use on the iPhone and iPod Touch. With the application, users can:

- Search for books, music, and more in the online catalog
- Read brief reviews or summaries for items in the catalog (when available)
- Get hours, locations, and maps for all DC Public Library locations
- Place holds on items to pick up later
- Cancel holds or change the pickup location
- Find out what others are reading with Most Popular
- Get directions to the nearest branch—walking or riding

The application is available as a free download on the App Store. The Orange County Library System in Orlando, Florida, has also developed an application for the iOS platform,

OCLS Shake It! Their application is a reader's advisory application that enables users to discover books, audiobooks, and movies based on suggestions from the application. Users can filter suggestions by audience, genre, or format. Users can also choose specific filters to limit results even further. Once a suggestion is made, the user can click on the title and be directed to the online catalog for more information. The application even lets users open the detailed catalog record in Safari. The application is available as a free download on the App Store.

North Carolina State University Libraries is another library that has developed an application for the iOS platform. They created the application WolfWalk. WolfWalk is a photographic guide to the history of North Carolina State University. It is a location-aware application that lets users take a historical walking tour of the campus. Users can browse photographs by decade, places, or theme. The WolfWalk application contains more than one thousand historical photographs. The application is available as a free download on the App Store.

Although native applications have some advantages, and libraries are developing them to reach users on specific mobile platforms, there are some disadvantages. Those disadvantages include:

- Native applications need to be developed for each mobile platform.
- Applications developed for iOS need to go through an approval process before they are made available for download through the App Store.
- Development of applications can be more expensive and time consuming.
- Libraries may not have staff with the expertise to develop an application of this nature.

The good news is that there are ways to develop native applications for the iOS platform that do not require learning a new programming language, enabling developers to create applications with their knowledge of existing Web technologies such as HTML, CSS, and JavaScript. However, before anyone can begin developing library applications for the iOS platform, they must first become a registered Apple developer.

Developing Library Applications for iOS with PhoneGap

For libraries, or any developer, to develop applications for the iOS platform, they need to be a registered developer for the iOS Developer Program. This involves enrolling in the developer program and paying the current annual membership fee of ninety-nine dollars. Enrolling in this program allows libraries to develop, test, and distribute library applications to users on the iOS platform. In addition to enrolling in the developer program, certain hardware and software are needed. To develop iOS applications, you need to have a Mac computer and to install Apple's software development kit (SDK) and Xcode, which is the development environment. Apple has yet to release a version of their SDK or Xcode that is compatible with computers running Windows. There are ways to install Xcode on a Windows computer, but it is more complex and requires installing a virtual machine on a Windows computer. Xcode is available to download from the Mac App Store, or on the Apple Developer website.

PhoneGap

Developers can create applications for iOS without knowledge of or expertise in Objective-C. Several frameworks are available that enable developers to leverage their knowledge of existing Web technologies, such as HTML, CSS, and JavaScript, to create native applications for iOS and other mobile platforms. One such framework is PhoneGap, which is built on the Apache Cordova framework. PhoneGap is an open source mobile development framework that enables developers to use existing Web technologies to build applications with native functionality through the use of native application programming interfaces (API). The resulting applications built using PhoneGap are considered "nativelike" or "hybrid" applications because the layout is not done using the platform's native user interface (UI) framework. However, they are not purely Web-based because they are packaged within a native shell with access to a specific device's APIs and distributed through the App Store. What this means is that if you know HTML, CSS, and JavaScript, you can create applications for iOS using the PhoneGap framework.

To install PhoneGap, navigate to their website (http://phonegap.com/) and click on the Install icon. This will direct you to the install page with more directions on how to install the framework, as well as a list of all the previous versions. The first instruction is to ensure that the NodeJS (http://nodejs.org/) program is installed before you proceed with installing the PhoneGap framework. This program will enable PhoneGap to be installed using the Terminal application. Once that program is installed, PhoneGap can be installed using the command-line interface (CLI). The command-line can be utilized on a Mac computer with the Terminal application. Once the Terminal application is open, use the following command:

```
sudo npm install -g phonegap
```

This will install the PhoneGap framework onto the hard drive of a Mac. In addition to installing the PhoneGap framework, the Apache Cordova (simply known as Cordova) framework will need to be installed as well. To install Cordova, run the following command in the Command Prompt or Terminal application:

```
sudo npm install -g cordova
```

Once these frameworks are installed, applications can be created for iOS using HTML, CSS, and JavaScript.

Creating a PhoneGap Project in Xcode

To create a PhoneGap project for iOS, use the command-line interface. Open the Terminal application and run the following command, replacing the appropriate part with the name the developer chooses for the project:

```
phonegap create LibraryApp com.benrawlins.LibraryApp Li-
braryApp
```

This command tells PhoneGap to create a project folder (LibraryApp), what the package name is (com.benrawlins.LibraryApp), and what the project name is (LibraryApp). There should now be a folder named LibraryApp with a www folder that contains these files and folders:

- config.xml
- index.html (with included tags for phonegap.js script and CSS)
- index.css with basic CSS styles in the css folder
- index.js file with deviceReady handler in the js folder
- images folder

After the project has been compiled, it is time to build the project for the iOS platform. To do that, an additional command needs to be run. In the Terminal application, a command will need to be run within the application's project directory. To do this, navigate to the application's directory from the Terminal application and run this command:

```
cd LibraryApp
```

This may need to be altered a little depending on where the application directory is located on the computer. Once in the application's directory, run this command:

```
phonegap build ios
```

This command will compile the application for the iOS platform. Once the application is compiled, it can be opened in Xcode (the development environment) and developed further.

Now that you have installed PhoneGap, created a project, and had it built for iOS, it is time to get in and start configuring it for your library. Navigate to the www folder in your project and open the index.html file. The index.html file should look similar to the following:

```
<!DOCTYPE html>
<!--
Licensed to the Apache Software Foundation (ASF) under
one or more contributor license agreements. See the NOTICE
file distributed with this work for additional information
regarding copyright ownership. The ASF licenses this file
to you under the Apache License, Version 2.0 (the "Li-
cense"); you may not use this file except in compliance
with the License. You may obtain a copy of the License at

http://www.apache.org/licenses/LICENSE-2.0

Unless required by applicable law or agreed to in writing,
software distributed under the License is distributed on
an "AS IS" BASIS, WITHOUT WARRANTIES OR CONDITIONS OF ANY
KIND, either express or implied. See the License for the
specific language governing permissions and limitations
under the License.
-->
<html>
```

```
<head>
<meta charset="utf-8" />
<meta name="format-detection" content="telephone=no" />
<meta name="viewport" content="user-scalable=no,
initial-scale=1, maximum-scale=1, minimum-scale=1,
width=device-width, height=device-height, target-density
dpi=device-dpi" />
<link rel="stylesheet" type="text/css" href="css/index.
css" />
<title>Hello World</title>
</head>
<body>
<div class="app">
<h1>PhoneGap</h1>
<div id="deviceready" class="blink">
<p class="event listening">Connecting to Device</p>
<p class="event received">Device is Ready</p>
</div>
</div>
<script type="text/javascript" src="phonegap.js"></script>
<script type="text/javascript" src="js/index.js"></script>
<script type="text/javascript">
app.initialize();
</script>
</body>
</html>
```

This is the default index.html file that PhoneGap automatically generates when a project is created. Before you start editing this file, you will want to run the project through the iOS simulator. The reason for this is to ensure that the PhoneGap project has been properly configured. If PhoneGap is working, you will see a screen with a blinking label that states, "Device is Ready." Once you receive this message, you can begin to customize the index.html file and add other files to create the library application.

At this point, you need to determine what information to build into the library application. What will users want to have access to in the application? What features are essential to include? These are the questions, among others, that were considered when developing applications at the Ensor Learning Resource Center (LRC) at Georgetown College. Features that were considered essential to include in the iOS application were:

- Hours
- Catalog
  ○ Link to download separate iOS catalog application
  ○ Catalog search
- Research
- Ask-a-Librarian
- Library Directory
- My Account
- Campus Map

- Library Map
- Full Library Website

Features to include may be different for your library, but it is important to develop a list of things that you want to include and then proceed from there.

Before the application is moved into production, you will need to check the domain whitelist options. Domain whitelisting in PhoneGap is a security model that controls access to outside domains like Google or even the library's website. The default policy is set to allow all access to outside domains. The PhoneGap documentation recommends that developers formulate a whitelist and allow access to specific network domains and subdomains. To locate the domain whitelist, configurations are found in the config.xml file located in the project, not the config.xml file found in the www folder. Navigate to the bottom of the file until you see something similar to the following:

```
<access origin="http://127.0.0.1*" />
```

In this file, you can specify the domains and subdomains that you want the application to have access to. For example, if you wanted the application to be able to access Google, you would include the following:

```
<access origin="http://google.com/*" />
```

You can do this for any other domain that you want the application to access, such as the library website, catalog, and library database if the application links out to those.

In addition to building mobile websites, jQuery Mobile can be used in tandem with PhoneGap to build native applications as well. The jQuery Mobile framework is a touch-optimized HTML5 framework. Since PhoneGap enables you to develop native applications using existing Web technologies, you can use jQuery Mobile within the PhoneGap project to develop your library application. There are two options for using the jQuery Mobile files in your application. One option is to download the jQuery Mobile files and host them internally within the application in a folder located within the www folder. The second option is to link to the CDN-hosted files. If you choose to link to CDN-hosted files, add the following to the config.xml file:

```
<access origin="http://code.jquery.com/*" />
```

At this point, you will want to include any image files or customized CSS or JavaScript files in the www folder in the appropriate location. Once the files have been added, you can start creating the application.

To start building the application using the jQuery Mobile framework, you will need to strip out some of the coding from the index.html file. The following coding from the original PhoneGap index.html will need to be relocated with the <head> tag.

```
<script type="text/javascript" src="phonegap.js"></script>
<script type="text/javascript" src="js/index.js"></script>
```

The rest of the code between the <body> tags can be deleted. Now you can begin adding in the elements for jQuery Mobile. The Ensor LRC decided to link to the CDN-hosted jQuery Mobile files. To do that, the developer needs to include the following within the <head> tag:

```
<link rel="stylesheet" href="http://code.jquery.com/
mobile/1.4.2/jquery.mobile-1.4.2.min.css" />
<script src="http://code.jquery.com/jquery-1.10.2.min.
js"></script>
<script src="http://code.jquery.com/mobile/1.4.2/jquery
.mobile-1.4.2.min.js"></script>
```

At this point, the index.html file should resemble the following example with nothing in between the <body> tags:

```
<!DOCTYPE html>
<!--
Licensed to the Apache Software Foundation (ASF) under
one or more contributor license agreements. See the NOTICE
file distributed with this work for additional information
regarding copyright ownership. The ASF licenses this file
to you under the Apache License, Version 2.0 (the "Li-
cense"); you may not use this file except in compliance
with the License. You may obtain a copy of the License at

http://www.apache.org/licenses/LICENSE-2.0

Unless required by applicable law or agreed to in writing,
software distributed under the License is distributed on
an "AS IS" BASIS, WITHOUT WARRANTIES OR CONDITIONS OF ANY
KIND, either express or implied. See the License for the
specific language governing permissions and limitations
under the License.
-->
<html>
<head>
<meta charset="utf-8" />
<meta name="format-detection" content="telephone=no" />
<meta name="viewport" content="user-scalable=no,
initial-scale=1, maximum-scale=1, minimum-scale=1,
width=device-width, height=device-height, target-density
dpi=device-dpi" />
<link rel="stylesheet" type="text/css" href="css/index.
css" />
<title>Hello World</title>
<script type="text/javascript" src="phonegap.js"></script>
<script type="text/javascript" src="js/index.js"></script>

<link rel="stylesheet" href="http://code.jquery.com/
mobile/1.4.2/jquery.mobile-1.4.2.min.css" />
```

```
<script src="http://code.jquery.com/jquery-1.10.2.min.
js"></script>
<script src="http://code.jquery.com/mobile/1.4.2/jquery
.mobile-1.4.2.min.js"></script>

</head>
<body>

</body>
</html>
```

Now you will want to start creating the home page for the application by adding additional elements of jQuery Mobile code between the <body> tags. The following are the elements that the Ensor LRC added between the <body> tags to create the home page for the application.

```
<div data-role="page" id="home">

<div data-role="header">
<div class="lrc_banner" align="center"><img src="applogo.
png" title="Ensor LRC" alt="Ensor LRC Logo"/>
</div>
</div><!-- /header -->

<div data-role="content">
<ul data-role="listview">
<li><a href="http://www.georgetowncollege.edu/library/
mobile/#hours" target="_blank">Hours</a></li>
<li><a href="#catalog" data-rel="dialog">Catalog</a></li>
<li><a href="#research">Research</a></li>
<li><a href="#ask">Ask-A-Librarian</a></li>
<li><a href="#directory">Library Directory</a></li>
<li><a href="https://voyager.georgetowncollege.edu/vwebv/
login?sk=m" target="_blank">My Account</a></li>
<li><a href="map.html" rel="external">Campus Map</a></li>
<li><a href="#maps">Library Maps</a></li>
<li><a href="http://www.georgetowncollege.edu/library/"
target="_blank">Full Library Website</a></li>
</ul>
</div><!-- /content -->

</div><!-- /page -->
```

This page now has a header and an unordered list of content accessible through the application. With jQuery Mobile, you can create multiple pages within the same HTML file and link them. That is what this example shows.

```
<li><a href="#research">Research</a></li>
```

The above example shows that the Research list item will need to link to the research page (#research) that is located within the index.html file. Alternatively, if you wanted to create separate pages for each of the list items, then the list item code would be similar to the following:

```
<li><a href="map.html" rel="external">Campus Map</a></li>
```

The rel="external" attribute is required if linking to an outside document or website that is not located with the current HTML document. If this attribute is not added, then it will not link to any external documents or websites. After all the elements of jQuery Mobile are added, the index.html will resemble the following:

```
<!DOCTYPE html>
<!--
Licensed to the Apache Software Foundation (ASF) under
one or more contributor license agreements. See the NOTICE
file distributed with this work for additional information
regarding copyright ownership. The ASF licenses this file
to you under the Apache License, Version 2.0 (the "Li-
cense"); you may not use this file except in compliance
with the License. You may obtain a copy of the License at

http://www.apache.org/licenses/LICENSE-2.0

Unless required by applicable law or agreed to in writing,
software distributed under the License is distributed on
an "AS IS" BASIS, WITHOUT WARRANTIES OR CONDITIONS OF ANY
KIND, either express or implied. See the License for the
specific language governing permissions and limitations
under the License.
-->
<html>
<head>
<meta charset="utf-8" />
<meta name="format-detection" content="telephone=no" />
<meta name="viewport" content="user-scalable=no,
initial-scale=1, maximum-scale=1, minimum-scale=1,
width=device-width, height=device-height, target-density
dpi=device-dpi" />
<link rel="stylesheet" type="text/css" href="css/index.
css" />
<title>Hello World</title>
<script type="text/javascript" src="phonegap.js"></script>
<script type="text/javascript" src="js/index.js"></script>

<link rel="stylesheet" href="http://code.jquery.com/
mobile/1.4.2/jquery.mobile-1.4.2.min.css" />
<script src="http://code.jquery.com/jquery-1.10.2.min.
js"></script>
```

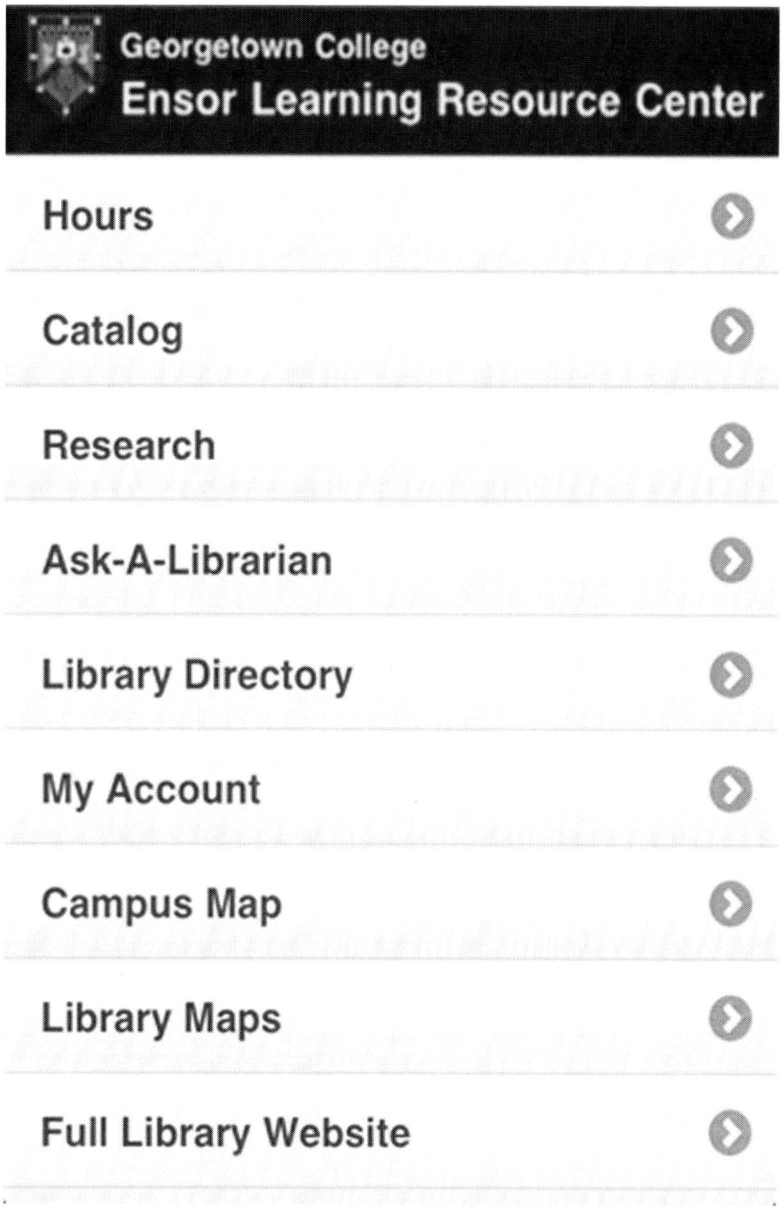

Figure 5.1. Screenshot of LRC iOS application.

```
<script src="http://code.jquery.com/mobile/1.4.2/jquery
.mobile-1.4.2.min.js"></script>

</head>
<body>
<div data-role="page" id="home">

<div data-role="header">
<div class="lrc_banner" align="center"><img src="applogo
.png" title="Ensor LRC" alt="Ensor LRC Logo"/>
</div>
</div><!-- /header -->

<div data-role="content">
```

```
<ul data-role="listview">
<li><a href="http://www.georgetowncollege.edu/library/
mobile/#hours" target="_blank">Hours</a></li>
<li><a href="#catalog" data-rel="dialog">Catalog</a></li>
<li><a href="#research">Research</a></li>
<li><a href="#ask">Ask-A-Librarian</a></li>
<li><a href="#directory">Library Directory</a></li>
<li><a href="https://voyager.georgetowncollege.edu/vwebv/
login?sk=m" target="_blank">My Account</a></li>
<li><a href="map.html" rel="external">Campus Map</a></li>
<li><a href="#maps">Library Maps</a></li>
<li><a href="http://www.georgetowncollege.edu/library/"
target="_blank">Full Library Website</a></li>
</ul>
</div><!-- /content -->

</div><!-- /page -->
</body>
</html>
```

The result of the above example is shown in figure 5.1. The features that you add to your library application will be somewhat different depending on what you as the developer feel is important. Once the coding is complete, the application can be tested using the iOS simulator, but at some point the application needs to be tested on an actual iOS device.

Testing an Application on an iOS Device

In order to test an application on an iOS device, the device needs to be to properly provisioned. This involves a process that requires the creation of a certificate signing request, a development certificate, adding a device, creating an App ID, and configuring the project to run on a device. The provisioning process starts with the creation of an iOS Development Certificate. A development certificate creates a secret private key and a shared public key that is similar to SSL certificates for securing a website. The first step to obtain the development certificate is to create a certificate signing request, which can be done using the Keychain Access utility. The Keychain Access utility is located in the Utilities folder, which is located in the Application folder. Once Keychain Access is open, navigate to the menu and select *Certificate Assistant*. Choose the option *Request a Certificate from a Certificate Authority*. A form will pop up. Fill out the form with the e-mail address and name that is associated with the Apple developer account that is being used. Leave the *CA Email Address* blank and make sure to select the option *Saved to disk* to save the certificate signing request to a specified location on your system. Leave the checkbox *Let me specify key pair information* unchecked. The certificate signing request should have been created and saved in the specified location. Both the public and private key will have been added to the Keys category in Keychain Access.

Now that the certificate signing request has been created and saved, navigate to the iOS Development Center (https://developer.apple.com). On the right-hand side of the screen, click on *Certificates, Identifiers & Profiles*. Under the iOS Apps section, click on the *Certificates* option. The options listed will be All, Pending, Development, and Production. Choose *Development*. To create a development certificate and upload the certificate signing request, click on the + icon in the upper right-hand corner. A screen will appear asking *What type of certificate do you need?* Under Development, choose the *iOS App Development* option and click *Continue* at the bottom of the screen. The next screen will have directions on how to create the certificate signing request, which should have been completed previously. Click *Continue* to navigate to the next screen. This screen is where the certificate signing request will be uploaded. Click on *Choose File* and find where the certificate signing request is saved. Upload the certificate and click *Submit*. Navigate back to the Development section and the development certificate will appear with a status of *Pending Issuance*. The status will soon switch to *Issued*, and the development certificate will be available to download. Click *Download*, and the development certificate will be added to Keychain Access under the Certificates category. The development certificate is valid for one year.

The next step is to add a device or devices to use for development. The easiest way to add a device is to launch Xcode. Once Xcode has been launched successfully, connect the device that will be used for development to your Mac. The Organizer window will pop up with the details of the device, such as the name of the device (e.g., Ensor LRC iPad), capacity, model, serial number, ECID, identifier, and software version (figure 5.2). Since this is the first time the device will be used for development, there will be a button that says *Use for Development*. Click on the button. Once it is clicked, a window will appear asking to add the device to a development team to use for provisioning. Click on the desired option and click *Choose*. Xcode will then prepare the device for development by downloading all the provisioning profiles needed.

At this point, the App ID for the application needs to be created. The App ID is an identifier that uniquely identifies an application in iOS; it is used by the operating system

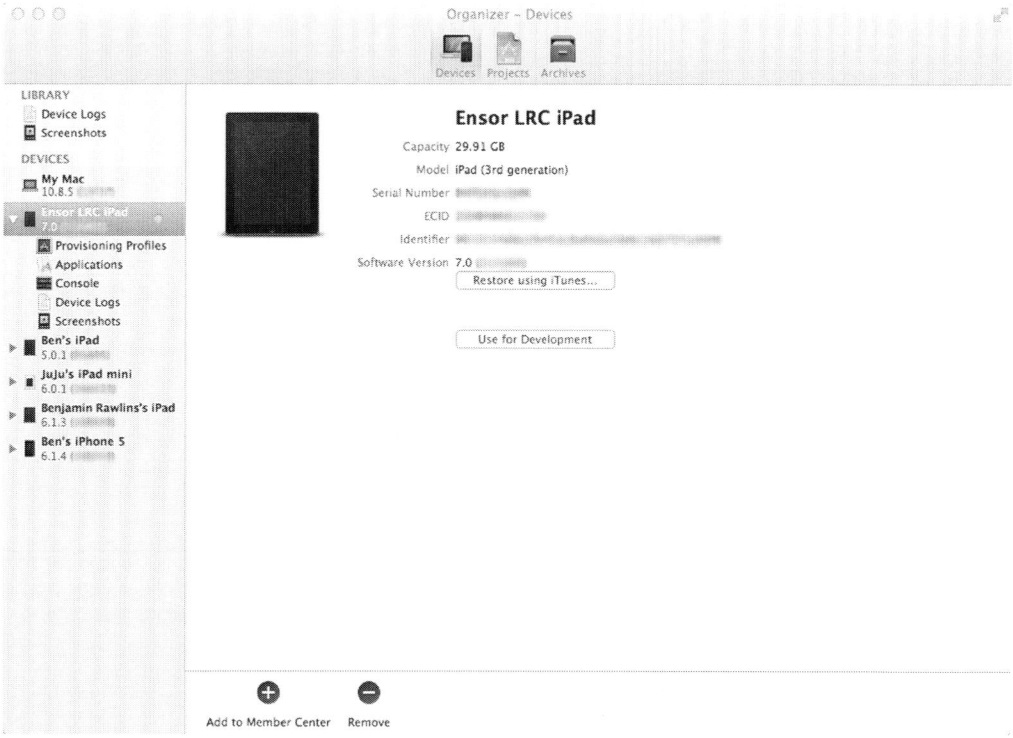

Figure 5.2. Organizer window.

for security purposes. To register an App ID, navigate back to the Certificates, Identifiers & Profiles section of the iOS Developer Center. Click on the *Identifiers* option and then choose *App IDs*. To register a new App ID, click on the + in the upper right-hand corner. An App ID Description, App ID Prefix, and App ID Suffix will need to be added. The App ID Description is where the name of the application will be added. The App ID Prefix value is the Team ID that is associated with the developer account. The App ID Suffix is the bundle identifier for the App ID and needs to be the same as when the project was first set up (e.g., com.benrawlins.LibraryApp). There are two options in the App ID Suffix section: Explicit App ID and Wildcard App ID. Select the Explicit App ID option. Once these steps are completed, the App ID has been created.

The provisioning profile is the next piece of the puzzle. Apple's documentation defines a provisioning profile as a collection of assets that uniquely ties developers and devices to an authorized iOS Development Team and enables the device to be used for testing. In essence, it is the profile that the iOS operating system needs in order to verify that an application is permitted to run on a specific device. To create a provisioning profile for development, click on *Provisioning Profiles* in the iOS Development Center. Choose *Development*, and click on the + in the top right-hand corner of the screen. An option will appear asking what type of provisioning profile you need. Select *iOS App Development*. On the next screen, the development provisioning profile will be associated with the App ID that was just created. The developer will then select the certificates that are to be included with the provisioning profile. The iOS Development Certificate should be included with the provisioning profile. The iOS Developer Center will then create the development provisioning profile. Once the provisioning profile is created, download it. This will prompt Xcode to open. Xcode will install the provisioning profile in Organizer. It will also install the provisioning profile on any device that is connected to the Mac.

Configuring the project is the last step before an application can be tested on an iOS device. For a project to run on a device, the build settings need to be properly configured. Open the Xcode project and click on the project from the Project Navigator panel on the left. In the Editor area (the middle pane) at the top left, there will be the application name with two arrows. Click on one of the arrows and select the only option that is available as a target (e.g., LibraryApp). Then click on the *Build Settings* option. Scroll to the section labeled Code Signing. In Code Signing Identity set the Debug configuration to match the provisioning profile that was just created. The Release configuration can be left to *Don't Code Sign*. The configuration should look similar to figure 5.3.

Now that all the steps have been taken to provision the device, the last step is to build and run the application. To run an application on a provisioned device, make sure that the scheme is set to a device, not the iOS Simulator. The scheme can be found in the top

Figure 5.3. Code signing.

left-hand corner of Xcode. Once the scheme is changed to the device connected, click *Run*, and the application will run on the selected device.

🌀 Submitting to the App Store

Once the application has been developed and thoroughly tested, the next phase is to submit the application to the App Store for approval. After the application is approved, users will be able to download it from the App Store. However, there are multiple steps that need to be taken before the application is ready to submit to the App Store for approval.

Prerequisites

Before an application can be submitted to the App Store, the project needs to have an App ID, a distribution certificate, and a valid distribution provisioning profile. At this point, the App ID has already been created, but the distribution certificate and the distribution provisioning profile still need to be created. The process to create both is similar to how the development certificate and provisioning profile were created.

The first step to obtain the distribution certificate is to create a certificate signing request, which can be done using the Keychain Access utility. The Keychain Access utility is located in the Utilities folder, which is located in the Application folder. Once Keychain Access is open, navigate to the menu and select *Certificate Assistant*. Choose the option *Request a Certificate From a Certificate Authority*. A form will pop up. Fill out the form with the e-mail address and name that is associated with the Apple developer account that is being used. Leave the *CA Email Address* blank and make sure to select the option *Saved to disk* to save the certificate signing request to a specified location on your system. Leave the checkbox *Let me specify key pair information* unchecked. The certificate signing request should have been created and saved in the specified location. Both the public and private key will have been added to the Keys category in Keychain Access.

Now that the certificate signing request has been created and saved, navigate to the iOS Development Center (https://developer.apple.com). On the right-hand side of the screen, click on *Certificates, Identifiers & Profiles*. Under the iOS Apps section, click on the *Certificates* option. The options listed will be All, Pending, Development, and Production. Choose *Production*. To create a distribution certificate and upload the certificate signing request, click on the + icon in the upper right-hand corner. A screen will appear asking *What type of certificate do you need?* Under Production, choose the *App Store and Ad Hoc* option and click *Continue* at the bottom of the screen. The next screen will have directions on how to create the certificate signing request, which should have been completed previously. Click *Continue* to navigate to the next screen. This screen is where the certificate signing request will be uploaded. Click on *Choose File* and find where the certificate signing request is saved. Upload the certificate and click *Submit*. Navigate back to the Production section, and the distribution certificate will appear with a status of *Pending Issuance*. The status will soon switch to *Issued*, and the distribution certificate will be available to download. Click *Download*, and the distribution certificate will be added to Keychain Access under the Certificates category. Like the development certificate, the distribution certificate is valid for one year.

The next step is to create a distribution provisioning profile. The process to create the distribution provisioning profile is similar to creating the development provisioning profile. To create a provisioning profile for distribution, click on *Provisioning Profiles* in the iOS Development Center. Choose *Distribution* and click on the + in the top right-hand corner of the screen. An option will appear asking what type of provisioning profile you need. Select *App Store*. On the next screen, you will associate the distribution provisioning profile with the same App ID associated with the development provisioning profile. Then select the certificates that are to be included with the provisioning profile. The iOS Distribution Certificate should be included with the provisioning profile. The iOS Developer Center will then create the distribution provisioning profile. Once the provisioning profile is created, download it. This will prompt Xcode to open. Xcode will install the provisioning profile in Organizer.

Configuring the project is another prerequisite step before an application can be prepared to submit to the App Store. Open the Xcode project and click on the project from the Project Navigator panel on the left. In the Editor area (the middle pane) at the top left, there will be the application name with two arrows. Click on one of the arrows and select the only option that is available as a target (e.g., LibraryApp). Then click on the *Build Settings* option. Scroll to the section labeled *Code Signing*. In Code Signing Identity, set the Release configuration to match the distribution provisioning profile that was created.

The last prerequisite step is deciding on the deployment target of the application. This is where you will decide the minimum version of the iOS operating system that your application can run on. This can be set to the current version of the operating system or to previous versions to allow devices that have not updated to run the application. Once the prerequisite steps have been completed, it is time to prepare the icons and screenshots that will be associated with the application.

Icons and Screenshots

Every application submitted to the App Store needs to have an icon and a launch image. Apple has set specific criteria so that the iOS operating system can properly display them. That includes what sizes the icons need to be and what file name they should have. To add icons to the project, follow the same steps used to code sign the project with the provisioning profiles. Instead of navigating to Build Settings, navigate to the General tab. The General tab is where the application's identity, deployment target, device compatibility, and device orientation are listed, and where you can add app icons and launch images. Scroll down to the App Icons section. When the PhoneGap project was created, the icons and launch images were created and added. However, these will need to be edited to reflect the customized icons and launch images for your library. Also in this section will be the icon dimensions as well as the resource name. When new icons and launch images are added, they need to be the same dimensions, and the file's name will need to be the same. The device that the application is intended to run on will determine what dimensions the icon needs to be. Icon dimensions need to be as follows:

- 57 x 57 pixels (iPhone with non-retina display)
- 114 x 114 pixels (iPhone with retina display)
- 72 x 72 pixels (iPad with non-retina display)
- 144 x 144 pixels (iPad with retina display)

All icons must adhere to the criteria above and must be in portable network graphics (PNG) format. Launch images also need to be in that same format as icons and have the following dimensions:

- 320 x 480 pixels (iPhone with non-retina display)
- 640 x 960 pixels (iPhone with retina display)
- 640 x 1136 pixels (iPhone with four-inch retina display)
- 768 x 1004 pixels (iPad with non-retina display, portrait orientation)
- 1536 x 2008 pixels (iPad with retina display, portrait orientation)
- 1024 x 768 pixels (iPad with non-retina display, landscape orientation)
- 2048 x 1536 pixels (iPad with retina display, landscape orientation)

To replace the default icons and launch images, click on the folder icon. Now the customized icons and launch images can be added to the project to replace the default ones that PhoneGap generated when the project was initially set up.

When the application is submitted to the App Store for approval, there needs to be at least one screenshot. Screenshots are important because they give the developer the chance to show users what the application looks like. Apple requires at least one screenshot and allows up to four additional screenshots. The requirements for screenshots depend on the targeted device. For example, if the application is universal, meaning it is designed for the iPhone and iPad, there will be separate screenshots for the iPhone and iPad. The required dimensions of screenshots are:

- 320 x 480 pixels (iPhone with non-retina display, portrait orientation)
- 640 x 960 pixels (iPhone with retina display)
- 640 x 1136 pixels (iPhone with four-inch retina display)
- 768 x 1004 pixels (iPad with non-retina display, portrait orientation)
- 1536 x 2008 pixels (iPad with retina display, portrait orientation)
- 1024 x 768 pixels (iPad with non-retina display, landscape orientation)
- 2048 x 1536 pixels (iPad with retina display, landscape orientation)

The screenshots from the application will be uploaded to iTunes Connect as part of the process to submit the application for approval.

Preparing Application for Submission

Before an application can be submitted for approval, the first thing that needs to be done is creating the application in iTunes Connect (https://itunesconnect.apple.com). Log in to iTunes Connect using an iOS Developer Account, and select *Manage Your Apps*. On the next screen, click on the option *Add New App* in the upper left-hand corner of the page. Now the basic information for the application will be added. The App Name will be the name listed in the App Store (e.g., Library App). The SKU Number is a unique string that identifies the application. Some developers use the Bundle ID (e.g., com.benrawlins.LibraryApp) or the date of submission (e.g., 01012014). The last step is to select the Bundle ID. The App ID that was registered on the iOS Development Center should appear as an option in the drop-down. Select the correct option and click *Continue*.

The next part of the process is to determine the pricing and the availability of the application. The availability date can be set for the date that the application is being submitted. Although it still has to go through the approval process, the app will be made available immediately after it is approved. After the price and availability have been determined, you will need to create the metadata for the application.

The metadata will consist of the application's rating, version, description, keywords, a primary category, and a support link. On this page the copyright information will also be included. There will need to be contact information listed. That can be an individual or an organization. The screenshots will be uploaded in this section as well. In addition to the screenshots, a large app icon with the dimensions 1024 x 1024 pixels will need to be uploaded. The large app icon is used to display the application on the App Store.

Once the metadata is submitted, a summary of the application is displayed. Under Versions, there should be the version of the application, status, and the date it was created. The large app icon will be in this section as well. Under the large app icon, click *View Details*. On the next screen, click *Ready to Upload Binary*. There will then be a series of questions about the application, and after they are answered, a message will appear that the developer is ready to upload the application's binary. The status will change from *Prepare for Upload* to *Waiting for Upload*. The application has now been created in iTunes Connect. The next step is to navigate over to Xcode.

To submit the application, an archive needs to be created. Make sure that a physical device is connected and that the scheme in Xcode is set to an iOS device, not the simulator. In the menu bar at the top of the screen, select *Product*. Once that menu is open, select the *Archive* option. Xcode's Organizer should automatically open and list the archive that was just created. On this screen, there will be two options, *Validate* and *Distribute*. Choose *Validate*. This will send the application through a process to check that all elements that are needed to distribute to the App Store are packaged with the application. If the application passes validation, it is now ready to distribute to the App Store and go through Apple's approval process. If it fails, there will be an error message listing the issues. Once those are fixed in Xcode, create another archive and repeat the validation process. After the validation process is complete, click *Distribute* and follow the directions on the subsequent screens to submit the application for approval. After the submission process is successful, the next step is to wait for the review process. The status of the application on iTunes Connect will change to *Waiting for Review*. This completes the process of submitting an application to the App Store. It is time to wait for the approval process to progress. There is no set time that it will take for Apple to review the application. It could take a few days or a few weeks. When it is available on the App Store to download, the status on iTunes Connect will change to *Ready for Sale*. That concludes the process of creating an application for iOS using the PhoneGap framework.

⑥ Key Points

A combination of the PhoneGap and jQuery Mobile frameworks can be used to create library applications for the iOS mobile operating system.

- Native applications differ from mobile websites because they need to be developed for each specific platform.
- The PhoneGap framework can be used to create native applications for iOS using HTML, CSS, and JavaScript.
- Applications for iOS must be approved before they are available on the App Store.

The iOS platform is just one mobile platform that libraries are building native applications for. The next chapter will cover how libraries can develop native applications for Android, another popular mobile operating system.

Reference

IDC. 2013. "Android and iOS Combine for 91.1% of the Worldwide Smartphone OS Market in 4Q12 and 87.6% for the Year, according to IDC." February 14. http://www.idc.com/getdoc .jsp?containerId=prUS23946013.

Developing Library Applications for Android

ANOTHER POPULAR MOBILE OPERATING SYSTEM is Android. As stated earlier, together with iOS, these two mobile platforms account for nearly 90 percent of the mobile market share. Using the PhoneGap framework, libraries can also build native applications using HTML, CSS, and JavaScript, just like they can for the iOS mobile platform.

Android

Google's Android is a Linux-based operating system designed for mobile devices such as smartphones and tablets. It was unveiled in 2007, and the first Android-powered mobile device was released in 2008 (Wilson 2008). It is primarily written in the Java programming language, which is different than Apple's iOS mobile operating system, which is written primarily in the Objective-C programming language. A big difference between iOS and Android is that Google releases the code for Android as open source under the Apache License. Apple does not release the code for iOS to any developers outside of their organization. The release of Android as open source allows the software to be freely modified and distributed by device manufacturers, wireless carriers, and developers. While iOS runs only on the iPhone, Android runs on a variety of different devices from different manufacturers. Android powers mobile devices by Samsung, HTC, LG, Motorola, and Sony, just to name a few. Amazon's Kindle Fire lineup is even powered by a highly customized version of Android.

Android is the most popular mobile operating system among developers, and it is a popular platform for libraries as well. A search of the Google Play store reveals that several libraries have developed applications for the Android platform; examples include the New York Public Library (NYPL) and UCLA Library.

The New York Public Library has created several applications for the Android operating system. They include NYPL Mobile, Find the Future, and HomeworkNYC. According to the description on Google Play, the NYPL Mobile application has the following features:

- Quickly search the collection, with filters to zero-in on the kinds of titles users are seeking
- Browse bestsellers and new material
- Get the details on any title, anytime and anywhere, including descriptions, community reviews, and commentary
- Check a title's availability
- Map the NYPL locations where the title is available now
- Place and manage holds
- Renew items
- Check location hours

The application is available as a free download. The UCLA Library Android application features the following abilities:

- Search library catalog and filter (keyword, title, author, subject)
- See description, availability, and location of items
- Find library hours and contacts
- See number of laptops available by campus location

The UCLA Library application is available as a free download on Google Play. An issue for libraries, especially smaller libraries, developing applications for Android, like it is for iOS, is that there may not be staff with the expertise to develop an application of this nature. The good news is that there are ways to develop native applications for the Android platform that do not require learning a new programming language and that enable developers to create applications with the knowledge of existing Web technologies such as HTML, CSS, and JavaScript. However, before you can begin developing library applications for the Android platform, you must first create a publisher account and become a registered developer.

CHAPTER 6

Developing Library Applications for Android

In order to distribute applications for Android through the Google Play store, a publisher account is needed. Although developers can still develop and test Android applications before this step is completed, it is recommended that this account is set up so that the account is already in place when it comes time to release the application. To register for a publisher account, visit the Google Play Developer Console (https://play.google.com/apps/publish/). If you already have a Google account, you can use it to log in; if not, then you will need to create one. At this point, you will need to enter the basic information for the developer. You will also need to read and accept the Developer Distribution Agreement. There is a developer fee of twenty-five dollars; however, unlike Apple's fee, this is a one-time charge, not an annual membership fee. Now that you have created a publisher account, you can focus on developing Android applications. To do that, the Android Developer Tools (ADT) Bundle needs to be downloaded and installed. It can be installed on a Windows or a Mac-based computer and downloaded from the Android developer site (http://developer.android.com/sdk/index.html). The ADT Bundle includes:

- Eclipse and the ADT plugin
- Android software development kit (SDK) tools
- Android Platform tools
- The latest Android platform
- The latest Android system image for the emulator

Once the ADT Bundle is installed, developers can begin developing applications for the Android platform.

PhoneGap

The PhoneGap framework can be used to develop Android applications without knowledge of the Java programming language and can be used to create applications for a variety of different platforms. To install the framework, make sure that the NodeJS (http://nodejs.org/) program is installed. This program will enable PhoneGap to be installed using the Command Prompt (Windows) or Terminal application (Mac). Once NodeJS has been installed, open the Command Prompt or Terminal application. Run the following command:

```
npm install --g phonegap (Windows)
sudo npm install --g phonegap (Mac)
```

In addition to installing the PhoneGap framework, the Apache Cordova (simply known as Cordova) framework will need to be installed as well. Cordova is the framework that PhoneGap is built on. To install Cordova, run the following command in the Command Prompt or Terminal application:

```
npm install --g cordova
sudo npm install --g cordova
```

In order for the command-line tools to work for Cordova, the SDK's tools and platform-tools directories need to be added to the PATH environment. On a Mac, the .bash_profile will need to be edited. The .bash_profile is a hidden file in the user directory on a Mac that contains the configurations and preferences for the command-line interface. This file can be edited with a text editor by adding a line similar to the following, depending on where the SDK has been installed:

```
export PATH=${PATH}:/Desktop/adt-bundle/sdk/
platform-tools:/Desktop/adt-bundle/sdk/tools
```

To modify the PATH environment on a Windows 7 computer, follow these directions:

- Click on the Start menu, right-click on *Computer*, and then click *Properties*.
- Click *Advanced System Settings* in the column on the left.
- In the dialog box, press *Environment Variables*.
- Under System Variables select the PATH variable and press *Edit*.
- Append the following to the PATH based on where you installed the SDK; for example, ;C:\Desktop\adt-bundle\sdk\platform-tools;C:\Desktop\adt-bundle\sdk\tools.
- Save the value and close both dialog boxes.

Java and Apache Ant may also need to be enabled. To determine whether they need to be enabled, open the Command Prompt and type the command java, and then the commandant. If they fail to run, append the following to the PATH environment:

```
;%JAVA_HOME%\bin;%ANT_HOME%\bin
```

Once these frameworks are properly installed, applications can be created using HTML, CSS, and JavaScript for the Android operating system.

Creating a PhoneGap Project for Android

To create a PhoneGap project for Android, use the command-line interface. Open the Command Prompt or Terminal application and run the following command or a variation depending on the name the developer chooses for the project:

```
phonegap create LibraryApp com.benrawlins.LibraryApp
LibraryApp
```

This command tells PhoneGap to create a project folder (LibraryApp), what the package name is (com.benrawlins.LibraryApp), and what the project name is (LibraryApp). There should now be a folder named LibraryApp with a www folder that contains these files and folders:

- config.xml
- index.html (with included tags for phonegap.js script and CSS)
- index.css with basic CSS styles in the css folder
- index.js file with deviceReady handler in the js folder
- images folder

After the project has been compiled, it will need to be built for the Android platform. To do that, an additional command needs to be run. In the Command Prompt or Terminal application, you will need to run a command within the application's project directory. To navigate to the application's directory from the Command Prompt or Terminal application, run this command:

```
cd LibraryApp
```

This may need to be altered a little depending on where the application directory is located on the computer. Once in the application's directory, run this command:

```
phonegap build android
```

This command will compile the application for the Android platform. Once the application is compiled, it can be opened in Eclipse (the development environment) and developed further.

To open the project in Eclipse, navigate to where the ADT Bundle is installed and click on the Eclipse folder. The Eclipse application is in this folder. Open Eclipse and specify the location of your workspace. Once in Eclipse, you will need to import the project by clicking on *File* and then selecting the *Import* option. A pop-up window will appear (figure 6.1). Select the *Android* option and then click on *Existing Android Code*

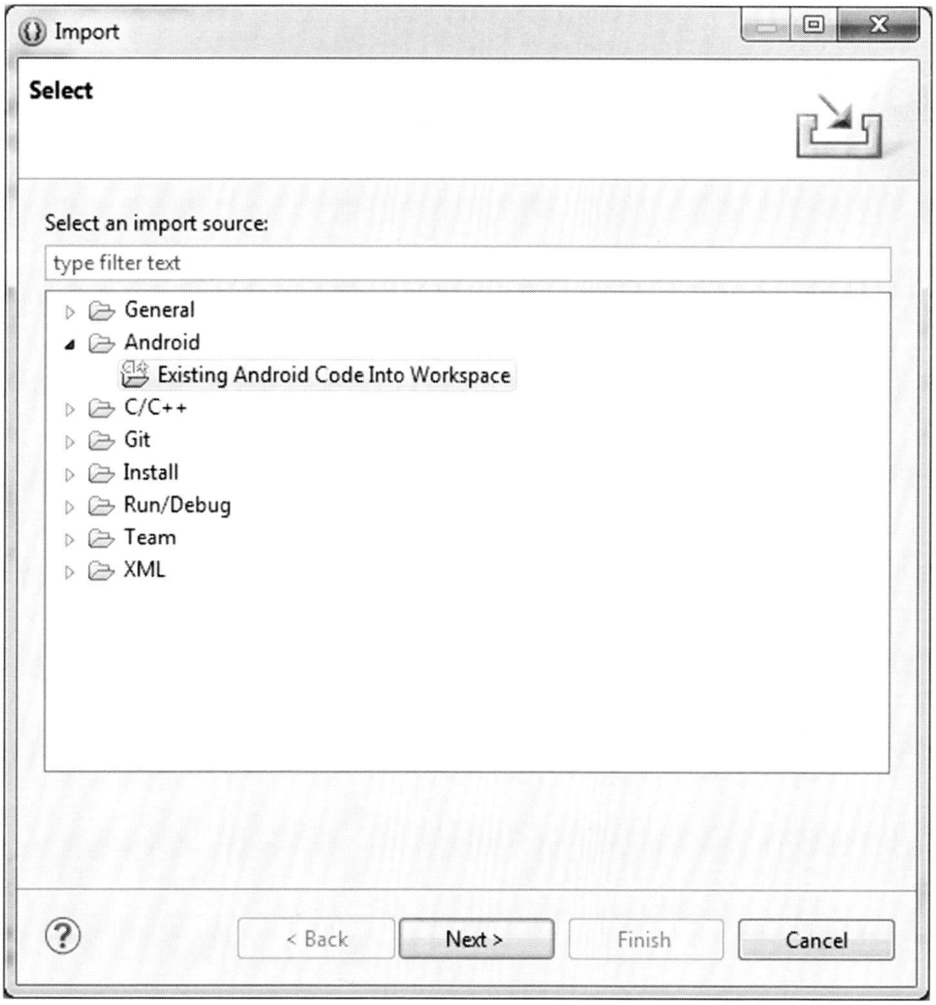

Figure 6.1. Importing project code.

into Workspace. Navigate to the root directory of the project and select the project folder. Once the project is selected, click *Finish* to import it into Eclipse. To continue to develop the project you just imported, go to the assets folder, which is where the www folder is located. Touch-optimized frameworks such as jQuery Mobile can be used to develop applications in Eclipse, just as they can in Xcode.

Building the Library Application

Now that you have installed PhoneGap, created a project, and had it built for Android, it is time to start configuring it for your library. Navigate to the www folder in your project and open the index.html file. The index.html file should look similar to the following:

```
<!DOCTYPE html>
<!--
Licensed to the Apache Software Foundation (ASF) under
one or more contributor license agreements. See the NOTICE
file distributed with this work for additional information
regarding copyright ownership. The ASF licenses this file
to you under the Apache License, Version 2.0 (the "Li-
cense"); you may not use this file except in compliance
with the License. You may obtain a copy of the License at

http://www.apache.org/licenses/LICENSE-2.0

Unless required by applicable law or agreed to in writing,
software distributed under the License is distributed on
an "AS IS" BASIS, WITHOUT WARRANTIES OR CONDITIONS OF ANY
KIND, either express or implied. See the License for the
specific language governing permissions and limitations
under the License.
-->
<html>
<head>
<meta charset="utf-8" />
<meta name="format-detection" content="telephone=no" />
<meta name="viewport" content="user-scalable=no,
initial-scale=1, maximum-scale=1, minimum-scale=1,
width=device-width, height=device-height, target-density
dpi=device-dpi" />
<link rel="stylesheet" type="text/css" href="css/index.
css" />
<title>Hello World</title>
</head>
<body>
<div class="app">
<h1>PhoneGap</h1>
<div id="deviceready" class="blink">
```

```
<p class="event listening">Connecting to Device</p>
<p class="event received">Device is Ready</p>
</div>
</div>
<script type="text/javascript" src="phonegap.js"></script>
<script type="text/javascript" src="js/index.js"></script>
<script type="text/javascript">
app.initialize();
</script>
</body>
</html>
```

This is the default index.html file that PhoneGap automatically generates when a project is created. Before you start editing this file, you will want to run the project through the Android emulator to ensure that the PhoneGap project has been properly configured. If PhoneGap is working, you will see a screen with a blinking label that states, "Device is Ready." Once this message is received, you can proceed to customize the index.html file and add other files to create your library application.

At this point, you will need to determine what essential elements need to be included in your application. The Ensor Learning Resource Center (LRC) at Georgetown College included many of the same features from the iOS application in the Android application to create a similar experience across both platforms. The features that the Ensor LRC staff felt were important to include in the Android application were:

- Hours
- Catalog
- Research
- Ask-a-Librarian
- Library Directory
- My Account
- Campus Map
- Library Map
- Full Library Website

You may select different features for your library, but it is important first to develop a list of things that you want to include and then proceed from there.

Before your application is moved into production, you will need to check the domain whitelist options. Domain whitelisting in PhoneGap is a security model that controls access to outside domains like Google or even the library's website. The default policy is set to allow all access to outside domains. The PhoneGap documentation recommends that developers formulate a whitelist and allow access to specific network domains and subdomains. The domain whitelist configurations are found in the config.xml file located in res/xml/config.xml, not the config.xml file found in the res folder in the www folder. Navigate to the bottom of the file until you see something similar to the following:

```
<access origin="http://127.0.0.1*" />
```

In this file, you can specify the domains and subdomains that you want the application to have access to. For example, if you wanted the application to be able to access Google, you would include the following:

```
<access origin="http://google.com/*" />
```

You can do this for any other domain that you want the application to access, such as the library website, catalog, and library database if the application links out to those.

jQuery Mobile and PhoneGap

In addition to building mobile websites, jQuery Mobile can be used in tandem with PhoneGap to build native applications as well. The jQuery Mobile framework is a touch-optimized HTML5 framework. Since PhoneGap enables you to develop native applications using existing Web technologies, you can use jQuery Mobile within the PhoneGap project to develop your library application. There are two options for using the jQuery Mobile files in your application. One option is to download the jQuery Mobile files and host them internally within the application in a folder located within the www folder. The second option is to link to the CDN-hosted files. If you choose to link to CDN-hosted files, add the following to the config.xml file:

```
<access origin="http://code.jquery.com/*" />
```

At this point, you will want to include any image files or customized CSS or JavaScript files in the www folder in the appropriate location. Once the files have been added, you can start creating the application.

To start building the application with jQuery Mobile, you will need to strip out some of the coding from the index.html file. The following coding from the original PhoneGap index.html will need to be relocated with the <head> tag.

```
<script type="text/javascript" src="phonegap.js"></script>
<script type="text/javascript" src="js/index.js"></script>
```

The rest of the code between the <body> tags can be deleted. Now you can begin adding in the elements for jQuery Mobile. The Ensor LRC decided to link to the CDN-hosted jQuery Mobile files. To do that, you need to include the following within the <head> tag:

```
<link rel="stylesheet" href="http://code.jquery.com/
mobile/1.4.2/jquery.mobile-1.4.2.min.css" />
<script src="http://code.jquery.com/jquery-1.10.2.min.
js"></script>
<script src="http://code.jquery.com/mobile/1.4.2/jquery
.mobile-1.4.2.min.js"></script>
```

At this point, the index.html file should resemble the following example with nothing in between the <body> tags:

```html
<!DOCTYPE html>
<!--
Licensed to the Apache Software Foundation (ASF) under
one or more contributor license agreements. See the NO-
TICE file distributed with this work for additional in-
formation regarding copyright ownership. The ASF licenses
this file to you under the Apache License, Version 2.0
(the "License"); you may not use this file except in
compliance with the License. You may obtain a copy of
the License at

http://www.apache.org/licenses/LICENSE-2.0

Unless required by applicable law or agreed to in writing,
software distributed under the License is distributed on
an "AS IS" BASIS, WITHOUT WARRANTIES OR CONDITIONS OF ANY
KIND, either express or implied. See the License for the
specific language governing permissions and limitations
under the License.
-->
<html>
<head>
<meta charset="utf-8" />
<meta name="format-detection" content="telephone=no" />
<meta name="viewport" content="user-scalable=no,
initial-scale=1, maximum-scale=1, minimum-scale=1,
width=device-width, height=device-height, target-density
dpi=device-dpi" />
<link rel="stylesheet" type="text/css" href="css/index.
css" />
<title>Hello World</title>
<script type="text/javascript" src="phonegap.js"></script>
<script type="text/javascript" src="js/index.js"></script>

<link rel="stylesheet" href="http://code.jquery.com/
mobile/1.4.2/jquery.mobile-1.4.2.min.css" />
<script src="http://code.jquery.com/jquery-1.10.2.min.
js"></script>
<script src="http://code.jquery.com/mobile/1.4.2/jquery
.mobile-1.4.2.min.js"></script>

</head>
<body>

</body>
</html>
```

Now you will want to start creating the home page for the application by adding additional elements of jQuery Mobile code between the <body> tags. The following are the elements that the Ensor LRC added between the <body> tags to create the home page for the application.

```
<div data-role="page" id="home">

<div data-role="header">
<div class="lrc_banner" align="center"><img src="applogo
.png" title="Ensor LRC" alt="Ensor LRC Logo"/>
</div>
</div><!-- /header -->

<div data-role="content">
<ul data-role="listview">
<li><a href="http://www.georgetowncollege.edu/library/
mobile/#hours" target="_blank">Hours</a></li>
<li><a href="#catalog">Catalog</a></li>
<li><a href="#research">Research</a></li>
<li><a href="#ask">Ask-A-Librarian</a></li>
<li><a href="#directory">Library Directory</a></li>
<li><a href="https://voyager.georgetowncollege.edu/vwebv/
login?sk=m" target="_blank">My Account</a></li>
<li><a href="map.html" rel="external">Campus Map</a></li>
<li><a href="#maps">Library Maps</a></li>
<li><a href="http://www.georgetowncollege.edu/library/"
target="_blank">Full Library Website</a></li>
</ul>
</div><!-- /content -->

</div><!-- /page -->
```

This page now has a header and an unordered list of content accessible through the application. With jQuery Mobile, you can create multiple pages within the same HTML file and link them. That is what this example shows.

```
<li><a href="#research">Research</a></li>
```

The above example shows that the Research list item will need to link to the research page (#research) that is located within the index.html file. Alternatively, if you wanted to create separate pages for each of the list items, then the list item code would be similar to the following:

```
<li><a href="map.html" rel="external">Campus Map</a></li>
```

The rel="external" attribute is required if linking to an outside document or website that is not located with the current HTML document. If this attribute is not added, then it will not link to any external documents or websites. After all the elements of jQuery Mobile are added, the index.html will resemble the following:

```html
<!DOCTYPE html>
<!--
Licensed to the Apache Software Foundation (ASF) under
one or more contributor license agreements. See the NOTICE
file distributed with this work for additional information
regarding copyright ownership. The ASF licenses this file
to you under the Apache License, Version 2.0 (the "Li-
cense"); you may not use this file except in compliance
with the License. You may obtain a copy of the License at

http://www.apache.org/licenses/LICENSE-2.0

Unless required by applicable law or agreed to in writing,
software distributed under the License is distributed on
an "AS IS" BASIS, WITHOUT WARRANTIES OR CONDITIONS OF ANY
KIND, either express or implied. See the License for the
specific language governing permissions and limitations
under the License.
-->
<html>
<head>
<meta charset="utf-8" />
<meta name="format-detection" content="telephone=no" />
<meta name="viewport" content="user-scalable=no,
initial-scale=1, maximum-scale=1, minimum-scale=1,
width=device-width, height=device-height, target-density
dpi=device-dpi" />
<link rel="stylesheet" type="text/css" href="css/index
.css" />
<title>Hello World</title>
<script type="text/javascript" src="phonegap.js"></script>
<script type="text/javascript" src="js/index.js"></script>

<link rel="stylesheet" href="http://code.jquery.com/
mobile/1.4.2/jquery.mobile-1.4.2.min.css" />
<script src="http://code.jquery.com/jquery-1.10.2.min.
js"></script>
<script src="http://code.jquery.com/mobile/1.4.2/jquery
.mobile-1.4.2.min.js"></script>

</head>
<body>
<div data-role="page" id="home">

<div data-role="header">
<div class="lrc_banner" align="center"><img src="applogo.
png" title="Ensor LRC" alt="Ensor LRC Logo"/>
</div>
</div><!-- /header -->
```

```
<div data-role="content">
<ul data-role="listview">
<li><a href="http://www.georgetowncollege.edu/library/
mobile/#hours" target="_blank">Hours</a></li>
<li><a href="#catalog">Catalog</a></li>
<li><a href="#research">Research</a></li>
<li><a href="#ask">Ask-A-Librarian</a></li>
<li><a href="#directory">Library Directory</a></li>
<li><a href="https://voyager.georgetowncollege.edu/vwebv/
login?sk=m" target="_blank">My Account</a></li>
<li><a href="map.html" rel="external">Campus Map</a></li>
<li><a href="#maps">Library Maps</a></li>
<li><a href="http://www.georgetowncollege.edu/library/"
target="_blank">Full Library Website</a></li>
</ul>
</div><!-- /content -->
[half line]
</div><!-- /page -->
</body>
</html>
```

The result of the above example is shown in figure 6.2. The features that you add to your library application will be somewhat different depending on what you as the developer feel is important.

After the application has been developed further, it can be tested on an Android emulator and later on an Android device. To test the application on an emulator, a virtual device needs to be added to Eclipse. That can be done by clicking on the Android Virtual Device Manager icon located in the top navigation bar. Click on *Device Definitions* once the Android Virtual Device Manager is open. This will have a list of various Android devices. Select the device and click *Create AVD*. This will be the device that the application is emulated on. To run the application on the emulator, click *Run* in the menu bar. Select *Run As* and then *Android Application*. This will run the application on the emulator.

Testing an Application on an Android Device

At some point, the application will need to be tested on an actual Android device. Android devices can be used as an environment to run, debug, and test applications. The tools included within the ADT Bundle make it easy to install and run an application on a device. However, Google still suggests using the Android emulator to test the application on configurations that are not equivalent to those of the physical device. This allows the emulator to verify that the application functions properly on different versions of the Android platform, such as different screen sizes and orientations. In order to test an application on a device, there are some steps that need to be taken.

First, the application needs to be declared "debuggable" in the Android manifest file. This is automatically taken care of using Eclipse, because running the application from Eclipse enables debugging. The next step is to enable USB debugging on the device. On devices that run Android 3.2 or older, this can be done under Settings > Applications > Development. On devices running Android 4.0 and newer, it can be enabled under

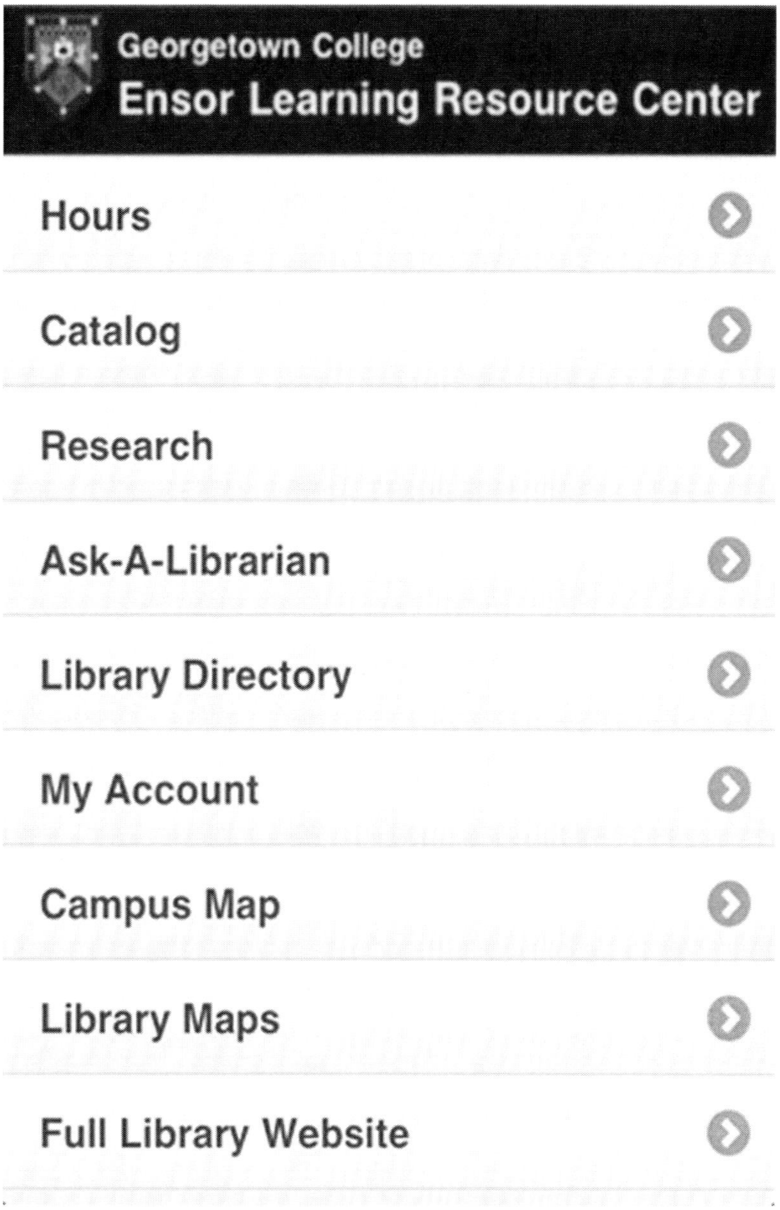

Figure 6.2. Screenshot of LRC Android application.

Settings > Developer Options. However, Google notes that on Android 4.2 and newer the Developer Options is hidden by default. To make it available, go to Settings > About Phone and tap *Build Number* seven times. The Developer Options will then be available.

Next, the system needs to be set up to detect the device. On a Windows computer, this means that a USB driver will need to be installed for the Android Debug Bridge (ADB). An installation guide can be found on the Android Developers portal for each original equipment manufacturer (OEM). On a Mac, there is no need to install the USB driver since it automatically recognizes the device.

Once these steps have been taken, the application can be tested on an Android device. It is not as cumbersome to set up a device for development for Android as it is for iOS. To test the application on the device, follow the same steps to run the application on the

Android emulator. You will be presented with a Device Chooser dialog box that lists the available emulators and devices. Select the device for the application to be installed on, and it will be loaded on the device.

Submitting to Google Play

After the application has been developed and thoroughly tested on the emulator and device, it is time to submit it to the Google Play store. However, before the application is ready for upload, you will need to ensure that you have added a customized icon set that follows Google's guidelines.

Icons and Screenshots

Since the application will be installed on a variety of different devices that have different ranges of pixel density, Google recommends providing the icon in multiple sizes. When an application is run, the Android operating system checks the device characteristics and loads the appropriate density-specific assets. The design guidelines refer to icon dimensions in density-independent pixel (dp) units. These are based on the pixel dimensions of a medium-density dots-per-inch (MDPI) screen. There are four primary densities: medium (MDPI), high (HDPI), x-high (XHDPI), and xx-high (XXHDPI). The icons sizes should be as follows:

- 48 × 48 pixels (MDPI)
- 72 × 72 pixels (HDPI)
- 96 × 96 pixels (XHDPI)
- 144 × 144 pixels (XXHDPI)

PhoneGap automatically generates some default icons. These will need to be customized to fit the needs of your library. Custom icons can be created and added using Eclipse by going to File > New > Other. A pop-up window will appear. Click on *Android* and select the option *Android Icon Set*. Make sure that *Launcher Icons* is selected and proceed. The next screen is where a custom icon set can be created within Eclipse. The generated icon set will contain an icon for each of the primary densities and will be added to the project. An additional icon will need to be created for Google Play. This icon needs to be 512 × 512 pixels in 32-bit PNG format with alpha and a max size of 1024 KB.

Google requires at least two screenshots of the application to be used on Google Play, but up to eight screenshots can be added for each phone, seven-inch tablet, and ten-inch tablet. The minimum dimension of a screenshot needs to be at least 320 pixels, and the maximum dimension cannot exceed 3084 pixels. Google also specifies that the maximum dimension of a screenshot cannot be more than twice as long as the minimum dimension. The screenshots need to be in twenty-four-bit PNG or JPG format (no alpha). Now that the icons have been created and the screenshots are ready to be uploaded to Google Play, it is time to export the application from Eclipse.

Exporting the Application from Eclipse

To prepare the application for submission to the Google Play store, it needs to be exported as an Android project from Eclipse. To do this, go to File and select the *Export* option. In the corresponding pop-up window, select *Android* and then *Export Android Application*. The next screen will show the name of the project that is being exported. Make sure that the correct application is selected and click *Next*. At this point, a keystore will need to be created. A keystore is equivalent to the certificate signing request that is needed for iOS applications. It is the file that will be used to sign and authenticate the application. To create a keystore to sign the exported application, ensure that the *Create New Keystore* option is selected. Choose the location that the keystore will be stored at and create a password. After this step is completed, click *Next*. Now that the location of the keystore has been selected and the password has been set, it is time for Key Creation. On this screen, there will be a form with the following options:

- Alias
- Password
- Password Confirm
- Validity (years)
- First and Last Name
- Organizational Unit
- Organization
- City or Locality
- State or Province
- Country Code (XX)

The whole form does not need to be filled out. The Alias, Password, Password Confirm, Validity (years), and First and Last Name are the only required fields. The validity requirement is how long you want the keystore to remain valid to sign applications. There is no set requirement for this entry. It could be one year or one hundred years. Once this form has been completed, move on to the next phase, which is to choose where the Android application package (APK) file will be located. The APK file is the file format used for the distribution and installation of software on the Android operating system. Once the APK file has been exported to a location on the hard drive, the application is ready to be submitted to the Google Play store.

Google Play Application Submission Process

To submit an application to Google Play, you need to be logged in to the publisher site in the Developer Console. Navigate to the Google Play publisher site (https://play.google.com/apps/publish/). A Google login is required. Once logged in, find the option to Add a New Application. A pop-up window will appear (figure 6.3). After creating a title for the application, the developer can choose to Upload APK or Prepare Store Listing.

It does not matter which option is completed first. Regardless of which option is chosen, there will be three options that need to be completed before the application is ready to be published on Google Play. Those options are Upload APK, Prepare Store Listing, and Pricing and Distribution.

There are three options to upload the APK file: APK for Production, Beta Testing, or Alpha Testing. In order for the application to be published on Google Play, the APK needs to be uploaded to Production. To upload the APK to Production, click on *Upload your first APK to Production* and navigate to where the file is saved.

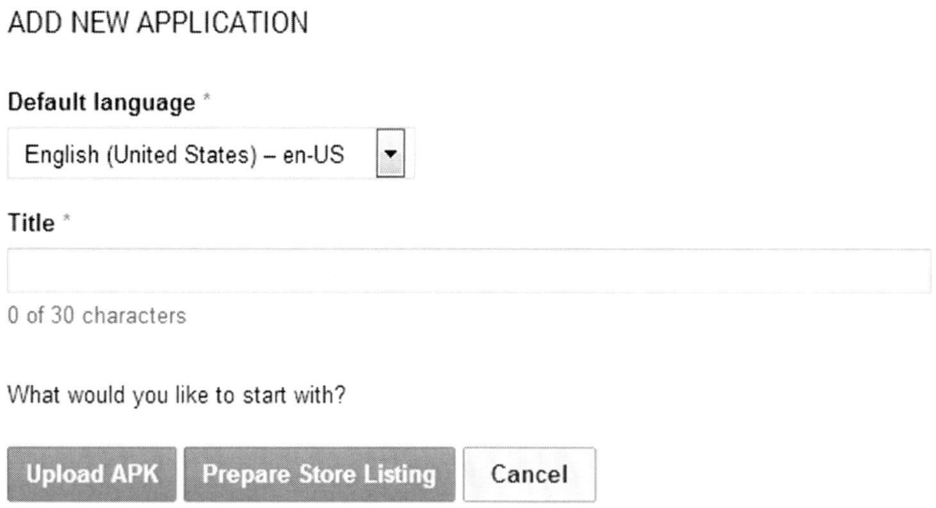

ADD NEW APPLICATION

Default language *

English (United States) – en-US ▾

Title *

0 of 30 characters

What would you like to start with?

Upload APK   Prepare Store Listing   Cancel

Figure 6.3. Add a new application.

To prepare the store listing for the application, there needs to be a description that does not exceed four thousand characters. At least two screenshots need to be added. If it is compatible with a seven-inch or ten-inch tablet, make sure to upload at least one screenshot for each. There can be up to eight screenshots uploaded for each device type. This is where the high-resolution icon (512 × 512 pixels) will be uploaded as well. Next up is the categorization. This is where the application type (applications or games) needs to be chosen, along with the category and content rating. Contact details also need to be provided, and these include a website and a valid e-mail address. The last bit of required information for the store listing is deciding whether or not to provide a privacy policy for the application. You can provide a link for the privacy policy or select the option to not supply a privacy policy at the present time.

The last thing to do in order to publish the application on Google Play is complete the Pricing and Distribution section. This is where you can decide whether the application will be free or if users will need to purchase it. The next part is to select what countries it will be available in. All countries or a set of specific countries can be selected. Additionally, to complete this section, you will need to ensure that the Content Guidelines and US Export Laws boxes are selected.

Once these three options are completed, the developer is ready to publish the application. There will be a green check mark by each option, and a button that says *Ready to Publish* will appear in the top right corner of the Developer Console. Click on the button and select the option *Publish this App*. This is all that is required to submit and distribute an application through Google Play. Unlike iOS applications, there is no approval process that the application has to go through before it is available. Once the application is published, it should be available on Google Play within a very short amount of time, typically no longer than an hour or two.

ⓖ Key Points

PhoneGap and jQuery Mobile can be used in combination to create library applications for the Android mobile operating system, just as they can for the iOS platform.

- Android is an open source mobile platform that appears on devices from manufacturers like Samsung, HTC, and LG.
- The PhoneGap Framework can be used to create native applications for Android using HTML, CSS, and JavaScript.
- Unlike iOS, Android applications do not have to go through an approval process.

In addition to developing library applications for both the iOS and Android platforms, library vendors offer a variety of other mobile solutions, which will be covered in the next chapter.

ⓖ Reference

Wilson, M. 2008. "T-Mobile G1: Full Details of the HTC Dream Android Phone." *Gizmodo*, September 23. http://gizmodo.com/5053264/t+mobile-g1-full-details-of-the-htc-dream-android-phone.

CHAPTER 7

Mobile Websites and Applications Offered by Library Vendors

OBILE WEBSITES AND NATIVE APPLICATIONS are a great way for your library to provide access to your services and resources. In addition to your homegrown mobile websites and applications, many library vendors offer mobile solutions. As a result of the continued expansion of mobile computing, library vendors have recognized the growing importance of mobile access to information and have developed mobile-optimized solutions to enable subscribers (and their users) to access content in a mobile-optimized format. Some vendors have focused on developing mobile-optimized websites that are accessible across all platforms, while others have developed applications to target specific mobile platforms like iOS and Android. A few vendors have done both. No matter what their approach has been, libraries and users are benefiting from these mobile-optimized developments. Mobile solutions provided by library vendors are a great way for your library to begin offering, or extending, mobile access.

Mobile Websites

Library vendors have taken different approaches to offering mobile access to libraries and their users. Some have chosen to provide mobile access through native applications for specific mobile platforms, while others have opted to develop mobile-optimized websites.

This section covers a sample of library vendors who have developed mobile Web interfaces as a way to offer mobile access.

EBSCO

EBSCO Information Services provides resources comprised of research databases, e-books, and e-journals to libraries of all types. EBSCO also provides access to content through mobile Web interfaces. Previously, EBSCO provided mobile access through a separate mobile profile, mobsmart. While your users can currently gain mobile access through this profile, EBSCO has developed an enhanced mobile interface. The new interface, dubbed EBSCO*host* Mobile 2.0, uses mobile detection technology to route your users to the appropriate version of EBSCO*host* depending on their device without the need for an additional mobile profile. Features of EBSCO*host* Mobile 2.0 include:

- Mobile device detection
- Basic search and results list
- Viewing HTML and PDF full text
- E-mail record with full text
- Multiple database searching
- Setting user preferences
- Guest access
- Integration with EBSCO Discovery Services (EDS)

While most of these features are available through either the mobsmart profile or EBSCO*host* Mobile 2.0, the latter does offer some additional features such as mobile detection, integration with EDS, guest access, and personal user authentication. EBSCO has sought to offer mobile access through a variety of different means, and they are currently one of the only library vendors that focuses on both native application and mobile Web interface development.

LexisNexis

LexisNexis provides a wide range of mobile solutions for subscribers. On June 22, 2011, they did a beta release of a mobile interface for LexisNexis Academic (LexisNexis 2014). If your library subscribes to this resource, then your users will be able to access the mobile interface for LexisNexis Academic through your IP range or via a proxy server. The mobile interface looks similar to the widgets on the Easy Search form on the full site. The mobile interface provides access to quick news and business and legal research. However, not all of the content is available through the mobile interface. The features of the mobile interface include:

- E-mail of full results lists or single documents
- Search the news (Today, 2 Weeks, 90 Days, 2 Years, and All Available Dates)
- Look up News Article
- Look up Legal Case
- Look up Company Dossier

The mobile interface is compatible with most mobile devices. However, if your users are accessing LexisNexis Academic with a Blackberry device, they may experience some difficulties, depending on the version of their mobile operating system. For example, if their Blackberry operating system is a version lower than 5, they may not be able to perform a search. In addition to offering a mobile Web interface for LexisNexis Academic, the company also provides mobile interfaces for Lexis Advance, State Net Mobile, Lexis.com Mobile, LexisNexis Communities, and LexisNexis Tax Law Community, among others.

Nature Publishing Group

Nature Publishing Group publishes journals with scientific and medical information. They provide journals and database the life, physical, chemical, and applied sciences, as well as clinical medicine. Their publications include *Nature*, *Nature Biotechnology*, *Nature Cell Biology*, *Natures Physics*, and many others.

To provide users equipped with mobile devices access to these resources, they have developed a mobile-optimized website. To access the mobile-optimized website, your users need visit your library's website and access the Nature publications. The website will automatically be reformatted for optimal viewing on a mobile device. This functionality is currently offered for the following journals:

- *Nature*
- *Nature Biotechnology*
- *Nature Cell Biology*
- *Nature Chemical Biology*
- *Nature Chemistry*
- *Nature Climate Change*
- *Nature Communications*
- *Nature Genetics*
- *Nature Geoscience*
- *Nature Immunology*
- *Nature Materials*
- *Nature Medicine*
- *Nature Methods*
- *Nature Nanotechnology*
- *Nature Neuroscience*
- *Nature Photonics*
- *Nature Physics*
- *Nature Protocols*
- *Nature Structural & Molecular Biology*
- *Scientific Reports*

The authentication process is the same as it would be for any other database or electronic resource. Your users will need to be connected to the library's network via Wi-Fi or use some other access control mechanism such as Shibboleth, IP access via a virtual private network (VPN), Athens, token-based access, or through a proxy server such as EZ Proxy.

The mobile website is currently supported on the iPad, iPhone, Android phones, Blackberry, Windows Phone, and a variety of tablets. Additionally, the mobile website from Nature Publishing Group is supported on mobile Web browsers such as Safari, Chrome, Firefox, Open Mobile, Opera Mini, and Dolphin.

BioOne

According to their website, BioOne is a nonprofit collaborative that was created to address inequities in science, technology, and mathematics publishing. More than 1,400 institutions subscribe to BioOne. The organization provides subscribing libraries with access to more than 150 journals. They provide mobile access to their resources through a mobile Web interface, BioOne Mobile. The link to the mobile website is the same as it is for the full website (http://www.bioone.org). If your users are accessing BioOne from a mobile device, they will be automatically redirected to the mobile interface. Features of the mobile interface include:

- Mobile-optimized interface for browsing, reading, and searching full-text content
- One-click access to your favorite articles and journals
- Filtering, searching, and sorting features
- Context-based searching for related research discovery

BioOne Mobile is currently accessible on iOS devices running iOS 3.13 or later, Android devices running Android 2.2 or later, and Blackberry devices running OS 6.

Your users can pair their device to BioOne Mobile through your library's subscription. If BioOne is accessed over the library's Wi-Fi network, then the device will be paired automatically, and a pairing code will not be needed. However, if your users want to pair their device when they are not connected to the library's Wi-Fi network, they will have to manually pair their mobile device. To do that, they will need to access the library's BioOne content from a computer, laptop, or tablet by logging in to your library's network and going to the following link: https://www.bioone.org/action/mobileDevice-PairingLogin. They will then be required to log in with their BioOne account or create a new account to obtain a pairing code. Once the pairing code is obtained, it will be valid for five minutes, in which time they will need to visit BioOne Mobile and tap on the Settings icon, where they will select *Device Pairing*. The code will need to be entered and verified. Once the code is verified, the mobile device will be paired with the account and your library's subscription access right for ninety days, after which the device will need to be paired again.

Web of Knowledge

Web of Knowledge is a research platform from Thomson Reuters that provides access to resources from the sciences, social sciences, arts, and humanities. It contains access to more than twenty-three thousand journals. The platform includes the following resources:

- Arts & Humanities Citation Index
- Biological Abstracts
- BIOSIS Citation Index
- BIOSIS Previews
- Book Citation Index
- CAB Abstracts
- CAB Global Health
- Chinese Science Citation Database
- Conference Proceedings Citation Index

- Current Chemical Reactions
- Current Contents Connect
- Data Citation Index
- Dewent Innovations Index
- FSTA
- Index Chemicus
- Inspec
- MEDLINE
- Science Citation Index Expanded
- Web of Science
- Zoological Record

In order to provide libraries and their users with mobile access to these resources, Thomson Reuters has developed a mobile website (http://m.webofknowledge.com). To access the mobile website, your users must have a Web of Knowledge user name and password. To create an account, they will need to log in to their library's network and access the Web of Knowledge platform and create a new account. This step is required to ensure that a user is from an authorized and subscribing library. Once the account has been created and verified, they will have access to the mobile version of Web of Knowledge.

Access to the mobile website can be achieved by typing in the mobile URL (http://m.webofknowledge.com) or by going to the full site URL. If going to the full site, your users will automatically be redirected to the mobile interface. The mobile version of Web of Knowledge has the ability to search within each of the individual resources included in the platform, as well as searching all the databases together. Other features of the mobile version include:

- Sort, refine, and e-mail
- Add records to EndNote Web
- Link to full text
- OpenURL
- View times-cited counts
- Citation score card
- Search history

In order to keep access to the mobile version active, your users will be required to log in to Web of Knowledge from an IP authenticated computer or device every six months to confirm that they are still an authorized user.

SAGE Journals

SAGE Publications is an independent international publisher of journals, books, and electronic media. Their resources cover a variety of different topics aimed at academic and professional markets. Those topics include clinical medicine, cultural studies, education, family studies, social work, and sociology. SAGE publishes more than 670 journal titles, all of which are now accessible through mobile-friendly interfaces. When your users access one of the journals from SAGE on their mobile device, they will be automatically redirected to the mobile interface. Their mobile site has been tested on a variety of different mobile operating systems and is compatible with iOS, Android, and Blackberry devices.

Although SAGE provides a mobile interface to their journals, not all of the features on the full site are available on the mobile website. Some features that are not available are Article Services, Share features, and About the Journal links. However, those features can be accessed by toggling to the standard site if a user desires. The features of the mobile website include:

- Browse tables of contents and online-first articles
- View abstracts
- Read articles in PDF and full text
- Search options across keywords, title, and author
- Hyperlinked references

To access the mobile interface, your users will need to be authenticated. To do this, SAGE offers a mobile vouchering service. The mobile vouchers allow your users to tie, or pair, their mobile device to your library's online subscriptions. To obtain a mobile voucher code, your users will need to use their device to visit the mobile interface and select *Authorize this Device*. Here they will complete the "Authenticate Mobile Device for SAGE Journals" form and enter the voucher code in the next screen and click *Get Access*. The mobile voucher grants them access to your library's subscription content for up to six months.

Annual Reviews

Annual Reviews is a nonprofit scientific publisher whose volumes are published each year for more than forty-one focused disciplines within the biomedical, life, physical, and social sciences. They have focused on offering mobile access through the development of a mobile Web interface. Access is available and optimized for most mobile platforms. The Annual Reviews mobile website enables users to:

- Browse journal subscriptions and articles
- Search journals by author, title, or keyword
- View article abstracts
- Access and read full-text articles
- Read forthcoming articles
- View and search references and related links
- Download articles to a mobile device for offline reading
- Share links and articles on social networks such as Facebook and Twitter

To access your library's subscriptions, your users will need to visit http://annual reviews.org from their mobile device while authenticated via a wireless network. If connected through your library's wireless network, a user's device will automatically be paired with the library's access rights, which will enable access to content from Annual Reviews while not on your library's network. The pairing lasts six months and is renewed each time a user visits the Annual Reviews mobile website. If your users are unable to pair their mobile device over a wireless network, they can log on to a network-connected computer and request a pairing code that will allow them to manually pair their device.

Taylor & Francis

Taylor & Francis is an international publishing company based in the United Kingdom that focuses on publishing books and academic journals. Taylor & Francis's mobile website will automatically detect what type of device a user is accessing their content from and redirect them to the appropriate interface. As a result, your users will only need to access Taylor & Francis Online from your library's electronic resources page or by visiting http://www.tandfonline.com. The mobile website supports most iOS, Android, and Blackberry devices, but if a user's device is not supported, they will be redirected to the full website. The features of the Taylor & Francis mobile website include:

- An optimized interface for browsing, reading, and searching
- Connecting to social networks such as Facebook, Twitter, and LinkedIn
- Access to a library's content by pairing a mobile device
- Creating a favorites list
- Saving full-text articles to a mobile device for offline reading

To access your library's subscription, a user can pair their device. The device pairing lasts for 180 days. If a user is authenticated through your library's wireless network, their device will be paired automatically. Your users can also manually pair their device in the same manner as they can for Annual Reviews. They can log on to a network-connected computer and request a pairing code from Taylor & Francis. There are detailed instructions on the Taylor & Francis website as well as a video demonstrating how to manually pair a device to access library-subscribed content.

While these library vendors have focused on providing mobile access through mobile Web interfaces, other vendors have targeted specific mobile platforms, such as iOS and Android, through the development of native applications.

Applications

Realizing that the mobile landscape is dominated by two mobile operating systems, iOS and Android, library vendors have chosen to develop native applications. This section contains a sample of library vendors who have chosen to develop applications for libraries.

EBSCO

EBSCO is one of many library vendors who have developed native applications. They developed an application for both the iOS and Android mobile operating systems. The application is free to download in the App Store and Google Play. To download and authenticate the EBSCO application for either operating system, your users need to navigate to the EBSCO database interface and look at the bottom of the page and click on the link that says "iPhone and Android apps." Your users then enter their e-mail address and get the following e-mail from EBSCO:

Dear EBSCO*host* user,
To begin using the EBSCO*host* iPhone and Android applications, follow the instructions below.

Step 1:
Download the app from the iTunes Store or Google Play
Step 2:
View this email on your device, then tap this authentication key
(**Note**: You must access the link in Step 2 from your device. The activation link will expire in 24 hours.)
Questions? Visit the support page or send an email to support@ebsco.com.
Thank you!
EBSCO Publishing

Once your users enter the authentication key, they will be able to access the databases through the EBSCO app that your library subscribes to. The EBSCO application enables users to:

- Choose which EBSCO database to search
- Limit results to full-text or peer-reviewed articles
- Get full-text results in HTML and PDF formats
- Save results for offline access
- E-mail results
- Automatically save the twenty-five most recent searches
- View an overflow display of results

Recent updates by EBSCO also allow users to save full-text PDFs to an outside application like Dropbox or iBooks.

American Chemical Society

The American Chemical Society (ACS) has developed a native application that is available for the iOS and Android mobile operating systems. The application is available to download for free. According to the descriptions in the App Store and Google Play, the features of the ACS Mobile application include:

- Up-to-the-minute access to new ACS ASAP articles, personalized across the entire portfolio of over forty peer-reviewed ACS journals
- Tailored "on the fly" filtering options for viewing content from selected ACS titles
- Delivery of an indexed list of more than thirty-eight thousand research articles published annually, complete with graphical and text abstracts
- Automatic saving of abstracts for offline reading
- A "Latest News" feed from Chemical & Engineering News Online
- Saving of favorites in a "My ASAPs" folder for convenient offline reading and pushing back to your usual research setting
- Interface to full-text article access (via wireless or virtual private networks) for users at institutions that subscribe to ACS journals; ID/password-based access is also an option for individuals who subscribe to ACS journals as part of their ACS member benefits package
- Caching of full-text article PDFs for forty-eight hours to read offline

- Quick Search across the more than 850,000 scientific research articles and book chapters now on the ACS Web Editions Platform—discoverable by author, keyword, title, abstract, DOI, or bibliographic citation
- Sharing of links and snippets via e-mail, Facebook, Twitter, and other options

In order for your users to authenticate and get full-text access to content your library subscribes to, they will need to be logged in to your wireless network or have an external login to access your library's system, such as a VPN login.

ebrary

Providing mobile access to e-books has been a goal of ebrary. In order to provide mobile access, they have developed an application that is available on the iOS and Android mobile operating systems. The ebrary application provides access to your library's e-book content. The application is available for download for free in the App Store and Google Play. The features of the application include:

- Online and offline reading
- Downloading of full titles
- Simple and advanced search
- Multiple navigation controls
- Table of contents with relevancy rankings
- Early check-in of ebrary's e-books
- Copy and paste with automatic citation for offline documents
- User-configurable download size warnings
- Import and use documents from other sources
- Available in English and Spanish
- Optional sign-in with Facebook user name and password
- Use of up to six different devices from the same account

Your users can authenticate and gain access to your library's collection of e-books by using the e-mail address they used to create an account while being connected through your library's network.

Naxos Music Library

Naxos Digital Services offers the Naxos Music Library application, which is available on both the iOS and Android operating systems. The Naxos Music Library database is a classical music streaming resource that allows users to access content from more than 90,000 compact discs that includes more than 1.3 million tracks. Content from over eight hundred compact discs are added to the resource every month. The collection includes music from genres such as classical, jazz, classic rock, and classic pop. Chinese orchestral music is also represented in the collection.

The application is available as a free download through the App Store or Google Play, but your users must have a personal subscription or access to your institutional subscription in order to access content through the application. Users who are using your library's institutional subscription will need to visit your library's unique Naxos Web page (e.g., http://mylibrary.naxosmusiclibrary.com), or access it from the library's Web page. Your users will then need to navigate to the Playlist tab and sign up for a Student/Member Playlist Account. Once the account has been created, your users will receive a confirmation e-mail with a link to activate their account. The login that was created for the Playlist account will be the one that is used to access the content through the application. Once logged in, users will be able to access personal playlists, institutional playlists, and Naxos-created playlists. Additionally, your users will be able to browse and stream the full Naxos Music Library collection.

LexisNexis

LexisNexis has a wide variety of mobile solutions for their subscribers. They have applications for legal research, new and emerging issues, practice management and marketing, and litigation. Many of the LexisNexis applications have targeted the iOS platform, with a few applications being available on the Android platform. One application that is available from LexisNexis is Lexis Advance HD. This application is designed specifically for the iPad and is only available on the iOS platform. There is also a version for the iPhone, which is Lexis Advance.

The Lexis Advance HD application is a tool that allows your users to access legal research from the Lexis Advance resource. With access to this resource, your users can:

- View and annotate documents offline and sync changes
- View alerts
- Access previous research results and search within those results
- Organize with remote access to saved files and folders

It is available as a free download. Your users must have a current subscription with a valid user name and password to utilize the application. This is just one example of an application that LexisNexis has developed. Other applications that they have developed include CourtLink (iOS and Android), LexisNexis Law School Q&A Series (iOS and Android), LexisNexis Legal News (iOS), Nexis News Search (iOS), Lexis Legal News Briefs (iOS), Mealey's Legal News (iOS), LexisNexis Tax Law Community (iOS), Lexis-Nexis Lead Alert (iOS and Android), Martindale-Hubbell Competitive Essentials (iOS), Martindale-Hubbell Lawyer Index (iOS), and LexisNexis TextMap App for iPad (iOS).

Library Ideas

Library Ideas is a global media company that is focused on providing digital media content to libraries. Two services they offer are the Freegal Music Service and Freegal Movie Service. In addition to offering this service, they have developed an application for each service that is available as a free download for both iOS and Android.

The Freegal Music Service application allows users to access more than seven million songs from ten thousand record labels that include Sony Music Entertainment. The application has a download limit of three songs per week.

The Freegal Movie Service application provides access to thousands of movies and television titles to stream. Like the music service, there are limits on the amount of movies that can be streamed by your users per week, which is three. Each selection carries a forty-eight-hour viewing period.

The authentication process is the same for both applications. Once it is downloaded, your users will search for and select their local library. If your library has subscribed to the services, they will be asked to provide a valid library card. Once they have logged in with their library card number and PIN, they will be able to access the content of the Freegal services that your library subscribes to.

Mango Languages

Mango Library Edition is a subscription product from Mango Languages that includes a variety of resources to help library users learn conversational language skills. Mango Mobile Library Edition is the application that the company has developed. It is available as a free download on the App Store and Google Play. The application works on iOS devices running iOS 4 or later and Android devices running Android 2.2 or later.

The iOS application enables your users to access the same resources your library subscribes to that are available in an online version through your library's website. Android users will have access to the same languages with the exception of languages that are written from right to left or languages with unsupported characters. Mango offers a variety of language courses for English speakers that include Arabic, Chinese, Croatian, Czech, Danish, French, German, Greek, Hebrew, Italian, Korean, Latin, Polish, Russian, and many more.

To use the application, your users will need to create an account with Mango Languages via your library's website. Those account credentials will be used to log in to the application. Additionally, the application will be updated each time a user logs in if they have Internet access.

OverDrive Media Console

OverDrive is a distributor of e-content such as e-books, audiobooks, music, and video. The content is delivered with digital rights management (DRM) protection and allows library users to download available content. They work with a variety of different publishers, including Random House, HarperCollins, AudioGO, Harlequin, and Bloomsbury. OverDrive hosts more than one million digital titles from these publishers. In addition to providing this service to a large number of libraries, OverDrive offers an application on the Android and iOS platforms for users to access their library's OverDrive content. The application is available as a free download in both the App Store and Google Play.

The OverDrive Media Console application is compatible with iOS devices running iOS 6 or later and Android devices running Android 4.0. The features of the application include the ability to search the OverDrive content your library has access to. Titles that are downloaded in the application are automatically returned once the checkout time has expired. Your users can create wish lists and place holds on items in the application. In order to use and access the content, your users will need a valid account with your library. To complete the authentication process, your users will select their library and enter their library card number. Once authenticated, they will have access to your library's OverDrive content.

Gale

Gale is part of Cengage Learning, which provides a wide variety of teaching, learning, and research solutions for libraries of all types. In addition to providing these solutions,

Gale has developed applications for your library users to access content from your library directly from their mobile device. One application that Gale has developed is AccessMyLibrary. There are different versions of this application depending on the type of library. There is AccessMyLibrary School Edition, College Edition, Public Edition, and Special Edition.

The authentication process for each of the applications depends on the version your users are accessing. For example, AccessMyLibrary Public Edition uses GPS positioning to determine the libraries that are within a ten-mile radius and then provides access to your users. The School and College Editions allow your users to select the school or college based on state location. Once a subscribing institution is selected by your users, they will be prompted to enter their institution's password in order to gain access to the resources. The Special Edition operates the same way as the School and College Editions. Your users select a participating library from a list and provide the specific password in order to gain access to the resources. Once authenticated through these applications, your users will have access to the Gale resources your library subscribes to. These applications are available as free downloads on the App Store and Google Play.

SirsiDynix

SirsiDynix is a provider of library technology solutions that include integrated library systems (ILS) such as Symphony and Horizon. Libraries currently running these systems have access to the mobile catalog application BookMyne. This application is supported on both the iOS and Android platforms as a free download to SirsiDynix customers. SirsiDynix offers libraries a wide range of customization options. The customization options include events and suggested links updates, social media integration, and visual customization. The events and suggested links updates allow for push event notifications and suggested links to your users through RSS feeds. Social media integration enables libraries to display Facebook and Twitter updates to users on the application's homepage. The visual customization options enable libraries to customize the look and feel of the application with custom colors, images, and interface tweaks. There are seven different visual customization options. The title bar image displays next to the library name in the top of the screen. The title bar color can be customized, but the color value must be provided as RGB values. The background color can be customized, and the color must also be provided as RGB values. The library information button is where you would choose whether to place a button on the application's home page that takes users to other library information. Your library can also choose the app icon that will represent the application on the App Store and Google Play. These are some of the customization features for the BookMyne application. The BookMyne application includes the following features:

- Search the library catalog for items by title, author, subject, or general keyword, and place holds on items
- Account management that allows users to receive notifications and view checked out items, holds, fines, and other account information
- Managing bookshelves and allowing users to add books, CDs, DVDs, and other media to their bookshelves for reading later or to recommend to friends
- Find suggested reading

- Search by barcode by using the camera on the mobile device to scan the barcode on a book, CD, DVD, or other item and see if that item is available at the user's library
- Search and find libraries by name or address, browse a list of nearby libraries, or locate a library through a GPS-enabled interactive map

The application also includes French, German, Spanish, and Arabic language versions as well. Libraries that have customized the application to fit their needs are the University of Southern California Libraries, Calgary Public Library, Westchester Library System, and A. K. Smiley Public Library.

Boopsie

If your library wants to develop a native application but does not have the skillset, Boopsie for Libraries can help. They build custom-branded applications for libraries. Boopsie was founded in Silicon Valley in 2006, and according to their website, they have provided this service to more than 2,500 public and academic libraries. They have also developed applications for library-related conferences such as the Library and Information Technology Association's National Forum. The applications that Boopsie creates for libraries are downloadable on a variety of different mobile devices and platforms, including Android, iOS, Windows Phone 8, Windows Mobile, Kindle Fire, Blackberry, Palm, J2ME, and Symbian Series 600.

Boopsie applications for libraries include features such as an integrated catalog search that allows users to search the catalog from their mobile device. A library locator with GPS-aware technology is included that searches for branch locations, hours of operations, and contact information. The application integrates e-content delivery for e-books and video content. Users are able to manage their accounts, which includes placing holds and renewing items, through the application with ILS integration. The Ask-a-Librarian feature is included, which allows libraries to extend reference services to mobile devices with integration for text messaging, e-mail, phone, or library location information. Another feature included in a Boopsie-developed application is social media integration that allows users to stay current with the latest news and announcements from their library. In addition to providing these features, Boopsie also provides a website where libraries and their users can demo the application before it is downloaded on their device.

Boopsie helps libraries that do not have the staff to develop applications deploy native applications. They also stay current on mobile technology and maintain the application. The application integrates with a variety of different integrated library systems. The service provided by Boopsie has been used by a variety of different libraries, including the Seattle Public Library, Centre College in Kentucky, San Diego Public Library, and the Charlotte Mecklenburg Library. Boopsie is a library vendor whose focus is on providing mobile solutions for libraries of all types.

These have been just a few examples of library vendors that have focused on providing mobile access to content that libraries subscribe to. Some have chosen to develop mobile Web interfaces that are accessible across a wide range of devices and operating systems, while others have chosen to target specific mobile platforms. One thing is certain—library vendors have realized the importance of mobile technology and have started to focus more on providing access to content in various mobile-optimized formats.

🌀 Key Points

In addition to developing mobile websites and applications, your library has access to a variety of mobile resources provided by vendors.

- Vendors such as EBSCO, BioOne, Gale, and Taylor & Francis provide mobile websites.
- Library vendors have targeted specific mobile platforms, such as iOS and Android, through the development of native applications such as EBSCO, LexisNexis, and ebrary.

In addition to mobile solutions provided by library vendors through mobile interfaces and applications, there are a variety of other ways that libraries are developing mobile solutions—and not only for patrons but for library personnel as well.

🌀 Reference

LexisNexis. 2014. "Academic Mobile Interface." http://wiki.lexisnexis.com/academic/index.php?title=Academic_Mobile_Interface.

CHAPTER 8

Mobile Services and Solutions for Users and Library Personnel

IN ADDITION TO DEVELOPING MOBILE WEBSITES and native applications as a way to target mobile users and their devices, libraries are providing mobile services and solutions to users in a variety of other ways. These services do not revolve around mobile websites or applications, although they can be integrated within them. They include getting users to interact with the library using the features of mobile devices, such as text messaging, or lending mobile devices to users. Not only are libraries providing these services to their users, but they are also looking to enhance the knowledge of the library personnel by providing them with mobile devices for certain job duties or functions. This chapter outlines additional ways that libraries are integrating mobile devices through services aimed at users and solutions and tools for library personnel.

While the development of mobile websites and native applications target the Internet connectivity and other features of mobile devices, librarians are looking at additional ways to incorporate services to connect to mobile users and, in some cases, looking at ways to put mobile devices in the hands of users. One way that libraries are enabling interaction with mobile technology is by lending mobile devices such as tablets, iPods, and e-readers to users. Additionally, mobile devices, specifically tablets, can be used to replace desktop computers for searching the library's online catalog, and they can also be used for library displays.

With the expansion of mobile devices, library staff are often consulted by users about useful mobile applications and research tools that would be valuable to have on their mobile device. Thus it is important for library personnel to maintain an awareness of the capabilities and applications available on mobile devices. Another way that libraries can use mobile devices is by taking advantage of built-in accessibility features. With accessibility features built into many mobile devices, libraries are able to use these devices to assist users with disabilities.

These are just a few examples of how libraries are using mobile devices to provide services to users outside of mobile websites and native applications. Now let's take a more in-depth look at these and other ways that libraries are offering services with mobile devices and how these examples may benefit and give your library a few ideas.

Text Messaging

Text messaging is a mobile service that libraries can offer to reach mobile users. The use of this service does not require users to have an advanced mobile device such as a smartphone or tablet. All that is required is a mobile phone with texting capabilities. There are a variety of ways that libraries can utilize the features of text messaging to offer additional services. One is through text message alerts. Text message alerts allow libraries to:

- Notify users of fines and fees associated with their accounts
- Alert users when holds that they have placed are ready to pick up
- Show when materials are able to be renewed
- Note when items are overdue

To sign up for text message alerts, users are often directed to a website or instructed to text a certain set of credentials or information to a specified phone number to enable text message alerts. All it requires is that users have a mobile phone with text messaging capabilities and a text messaging plan through their wireless carrier. Examples of libraries that offer text message alerts as a service are the University of Arizona, Multnomah County Library in Oregon, Rice University, and Douglas County Library in Colorado.

Another way that libraries can utilize text messaging is through a reference service called Text-a-Librarian. Two vendors that offer this service for libraries are Mosio and LibraryH3lp. These vendors offer libraries the ability to provide text messaging services without having a dedicated mobile phone. To use this service, users text a question to a specified number, either a telephone number or a short string of digits, and it is sent to a dashboard that librarians can log in to and respond on. Librarians can respond from a computer without the need for a mobile device of their own. This service is best used for quick and simple questions (no more than 160 characters) that can be answered with brief responses. According to a study, the top competencies that librarians identified as essential to provide this service to users were:

- Ability to compose answers to patrons' questions concisely, quickly, and accurately
- Ability to construct effective search strategies and skillfully search online information sources
- Ability to quickly evaluate information and determine the validity, credibility, and authoritativeness of sources
- Knowledge of information resources, especially online information resources
- Ability to interpret patrons' information needs within the limited context of brief text messages (Luo 2013)

Libraries that offer the Text-a-Librarian reference service include Oregon State University, Indianapolis Public Library, the University of Arkansas, and the Public Library of Cincinnati and Hamilton County.

Libraries are also integrating text messaging services into the library catalog. Users can click on a link in the catalog and have information such as the call number, location, and title of an item sent to their mobile phone. This allows users to navigate to the stacks with their device without needing to find a piece of scrap paper and a pencil to write the information down. Examples of libraries that have integrated this service into their online catalogs are Eastern Kentucky University and North Carolina State University.

Lending Mobile Devices

In addition to targeting existing mobile users through the development of resources and services, libraries are striving to put mobile technology in the hands of all users by lending mobile devices. While developing mobile services for users is a great way to extend library services, it targets one subset of library users. By lending mobile devices to users, libraries are making mobile technology available to their entire user base. It offers them the opportunity to familiarize themselves with mobile technology and could provide users with a way of testing a device before they decide to purchase one of their own. Although many libraries now lend mobile devices, the devices they are lending and the strategies used to lend them vary depending on the library. For example, some libraries lend tablets, while others may lend only e-readers. Of course, the opportunity to lend mobile devices may not be available to every library due to budgeting issues, but for those libraries that are able to lend mobile devices to their users, there are a variety of advantages.

Lending mobile devices to library users has many advantages. One is that it puts the technology within the grasp of your library's entire user base and affords those who would not normally have access to such technology the ability to interact with various devices. It also allows all library users to have access to mobile services offered by the library, such as access to e-books, mobile websites, and applications developed by the library and provided by vendors.

Libraries have taken different approaches when it comes to lending mobile devices. Some have decided to lend e-readers, others tablets, and some libraries have decided to offer a variety of different devices for users to borrow. Let's take a look at some examples of libraries that are lending mobile devices and what their approaches are.

According to the American Library Association's 2013 annual State of the Library report, 76 percent of libraries offer e-books and 39 percent are lending e-readers (Hoffelder 2013). One library that is lending e-readers is the Ensor Learning Resource Center (LRC) at Georgetown College in Kentucky. The Ensor LRC has six Amazon Kindles with Keyboard and six Barnes and Noble Nook Touch e-readers available for users. The strategy behind offering users both Kindles and Nooks was to make the EBSCO eBook collection available to users through the Nooks and load popular titles onto the Kindles for leisurely reading. Users can connect the Nooks to any of the public computers and download and transfer academic titles onto the device. The Ensor LRC requires users to fill out an eReader Loan Agreement form before an e-reader can be checked out (see textbox 8.1). Once a user fills out the form, a note is made in their account stating that they have signed the loan agreement and the form is filed away. After that step is complete, the user has the privilege to borrow e-readers from the library. However, the devices are only available for Georgetown College faculty, staff, and students.

TEXTBOX 8.1.

ENSOR LRC E-READER LOAN AGREEMENT

I, [the user], understand and agree to the following:

1. The loan period is two (2) weeks with no renewals.
    a. If the Kindle or Nook is lost, stolen, or not returned, a fine of $150.00 will be placed on my account.
    b. An overdue fee of $5.00 per day will be applied to my account if the Kindle or Nook is not returned on time.
2. The Kindle or Nook must be returned in good working condition.
    a. If the Kindle or Nook is lost, stolen or damaged while it is checked out to my account, I am responsible for the cost of repair or replacement fees of up to $150.00.
3. I will not download anything onto the Kindle. The Kindle must be returned with the same content loaded on it as at the time of check out.*
4. I will not delete existing content on the Kindle or Nook.
5. I will not attempt to register the Kindle or Nook to another account.
6. I will return the Kindle or Nook to the Circulation Desk attendant and not place it in the book drop.
7. I will not attempt to remove the Kindle or Nook's cover.
8. Future borrowing privileges will be revoked if I fail to abide by this agreement.

* Nooks may be used to download from the Library's EBSCO eBook Collection or the ebrary collection.

Hooksett Public Library in New Hampshire offers a wide variety of e-readers for their users to choose from. These include:

- Nook Classic
- Nook Color
- Nook Simple
- Nook HD 7"
- Sony Reader
- Kobo e-reader
- Kindle 3G Keyboard
- Kindle Fire
- Kindle Fire HD 7"
- Kindle Paperwhite

Users are able to borrow an e-reader for two weeks and allowed to renew the device one time, as long as a hold has not been placed on it. Hooksett Public Library requires that anyone borrowing an e-reader be at least eighteen years old with a valid driver's license and a library card that is in good standing. Like Georgetown College, Hooksett also requires their users to sign a loan agreement form. Additionally, users are not allowed to download any content to the e-readers. They may select content from the library Over-Drive service to have loaded onto the e-reader for them (Hooksett Public Library 2014).

The University of Louisville Libraries offers eighteen Amazon Kindles with Keyboard for their users to borrow. These devices are divided between two of the branch libraries. One branch is the main library, which has twelve Kindles, and they have popular titles loaded on them. The other branch is the health sciences library, which has six Kindles, and they have books related to medicine or biomedical-related fiction or nonfiction. Users can borrow these devices for two weeks with no renewals. Although users are not required to sign a loan agreement, by checking a Kindle out, users are aware of the user loan agreement that is posted on their website (University of Louisville Libraries 2013).

These are a few examples of libraries that have launched programs to put e-readers in the hands of their users. One advantage of offering e-readers to users is that they can add an element of privacy since nobody can see what a user is reading. Another is that an e-reader is portable and allows for multiple books and reading material to be loaded onto them. They can also get users more interested in reading by adding the element of technology into the reading experience. The intimidation of the length of some print books may also be eliminated, as users are not able to see the physical length of a book.

While some libraries have launched e-reader lending programs, other libraries have decided to launch tablet lending programs or lending programs for a variety of different mobile devices. Examples of libraries that have chosen this route are the L. E. Phillips Memorial Public Library, Oregon State University Libraries, Brooklyn Public Library, and North Carolina State University Libraries.

L. E. Phillips Memorial Public Library in Eau Claire, Wisconsin, was the first public library in the United States to check out iPads to users. They were able to launch this program due to a $50,000-grant from the Presto Foundation. The iPads are loading with more than one thousand e-books, ten audiobooks, and a variety of different apps. The library has included the following information in their catalog record for the iPads:

The iPad must be checked out and returned to the L.E. Phillips Memorial Public Library circulation desk. . . . Maximum loan period up to 14 calendar days. It is not renewable. Customers must be 18 years of age or older, and be current library cardholders in good standing. . . . Overdue fees will be charged for iPads not returned by their due date in the amount of $10.00 per day. . . . Any content added by the cardholder during their checkout period will be lost. . . . The borrower will be held responsible for all applicable replacement costs and processing fees, up to $1,020.00 for the iPad and/or accessories if lost, stolen or damaged while checked out to the borrower's library card. The library's iPad Borrowing Agreement must be completed with each checkout, acknowledging financial responsibility for lost, stolen or damaged equipment. (L. E. Phillips Memorial Public Library 2014)

As noted in the last statement from the catalog record, users are required to complete the library's iPad Borrowing Agreement each time the device is checked out. L. E. Phillips Memorial Public Library even extends this service to users who may not be able to physically make it to the library. Users who are part of their Home Delivery Service are able to borrow an iPad for twenty-eight days, but must sign the library's iPad Borrowing Agreement upon delivery or the iPad is returned to the library. This is a way of extending this service to all potential users. The library has stated, "The goal of the iPad lending program is to provide library customers with opportunities to gain familiarity and comfort with new technology that allows them to make use of alternative methods of enjoying the written and spoken word and to more fully explore the Internet and its vast resource" (L. E. Phillips Memorial Public Library 2011). They are not the only public library in their area that has begun to explore ways to lend tablets to users. The River Falls Public Library is currently testing several tablet devices such as the iPad Air, Kindle Fire HD, Galaxy Tab 10.1, Galaxy Tab 2, Google Nexus 7, and the Microsoft Surface (River Falls Public Library 2014).

Oregon State University (OSU) Libraries has focused on lending tablets to students, faculty, and staff associated with the university. The tablet devices that they have made available to their users are the Google Nexus 7 and the Google Nexus 10. In order to check out one of the tablets, members of the campus community must provide a photo ID. They inform their users that the location services are set to on, but users are able to modify the setting once they have the device checked out. The library does allow users to download personal content onto the devices with the knowledge that once the device is returned all personal information and user-installed applications will be erased. Although users are not required to sign a loan agreement form, the library has posted a statement on their website that states that the checkout of tablets implies agreement with the following by the user:

> I agree to pay all costs associated with damage to this tablet device or its associated peripheral equipment or its replacement costs should it be lost or stolen. I understand that the replacement cost for this device may be up to $240 [Nexus 7] / $550 [Nexus 10] plus the accrued overdue fine(s) and a $15 processing charge. (Oregon State University Libraries 2014b)

There are separate policies depending on which device a user wants to borrow. For the Nexus 7, no reservation is required; users can come up to the Circulation Desk and ask to check one out if it is available. The loan period is six hours, and it can be renewed if there are other Nexus 7 devices available. The overdue fines for the Nexus 7 are five dollars for the first half hour and ten dollars for each additional hour. For the Nexus 10, a reservation is required. The loan period is one week with no renewals. The overdue fine is two dollars per day. The devices come preinstalled with a variety of different Web shortcuts and applications. Shortcuts include the OSU Libraries home page, OSU Libraries 1Seach, OSU Press, OSU home page, and Library2Go. Applications installed on the devices by OSU Libraries include Dropbox, Evernote, Facebook, Netflix, Spotify, and Twitter. In addition to lending tablets, OSU Libraries also offer Kindles to their campus community (Oregon State University Libraries 2014a).

One library system that has decided to lend a variety of different tablets, among other mobile devices, is North Carolina State University (NCSU) Libraries. The devices are available to borrow for students, faculty, and staff. NCSU Libraries offer the following tablets for their users to borrow:

- iPad first generation
- iPad 2
- iPad fourth generation
- iPad Mini
- Kindle Fire
- Kindle Fire HD 8.9"
- Nexus 7
- Microsoft Surface

The tablets are available on a first come, first served basis from the main service desk at the D. H. Hill Library. Users are able to borrow a tablet for a four-hour period or one week depending on the device. The iPad first generation, Kindle Fire, Kindle Fire HD 8.9", Nexus 7, and Microsoft Surface can be borrowed for one week with no renewals. The iPad 2, iPad fourth generation, and the iPad Mini can be borrowed for a period of four hours and renewed once. NCSU Libraries lends other mobile devices to their users, including iPods and a variety of e-readers, such as Kindles, Sony Readers, and Nooks (North Carolina State University Libraries 2014).

These are just a few examples of libraries that are lending mobile devices to their users. As you can see from the examples, although many libraries are lending mobile devices, there is no consensus on establishing policies. Some libraries require their users to fill out a loan agreement; others do not. There is even a difference between libraries that require the user agreement. Some require the agreement to be submitted once, and it is kept on file, while others require a completed agreement each time a mobile device is checked out. Regardless of the different approaches, libraries are realizing the benefits of lending mobile devices to their users. However, one big disadvantage is the cost of offering such a service. Some libraries do not have the budget to begin offering new technology services such as lending mobile devices. Although this is not the only disadvantage, it is one that is often difficult for libraries to overcome. Despite this disadvantage, for those that are able to secure funding or have the budget to do so, lending mobile devices to library users is a way for libraries to afford a larger portion of their base access to mobile technology and the additional services available through it.

Mobile Devices and Accessibility

The built-in accessibility features of mobile devices, particularly tablets, allow users with disabilities to enjoy and interact with mobile technology. Mobile devices can be used in tandem with other assistive technology available at the library or as an affordable alternative if the library is unable to purchase assistive technology. Companies like Apple, Google, and Samsung have made a concerted effort to include accessibility features in the software of their devices so that the technology can be enjoyed by the vast majority of people. For example, Apple's mobile devices include accessibility features for users with vision impairment, hearing impairment, physical and/or motor challenges, and attention challenges or other cognitive and learning disabilities.

Features for users who are blind or have low vision include the screen-reading software VoiceOver. This feature enables users to hear what is on the screen and use gesture controls to navigate on the device. Other features for users who are blind or have low vision include dictation, which enables users to speak instead of typing by using the microphone from the device. The zoom feature is also helpful, using a built-in magnifier to zoom in up to 500 percent.

Features for users with hearing impairment include FaceTime, which enables users to communicate visually. Users can also select to turn on closed captioning when they are watching a video. Apple is reportedly working with companies that make hearing aids to make them specifically for iOS devices.

The assistive touch feature can be enabled to help users with physical or motor challenges use custom gestures to control their device. Guided Access is a feature that allows users with autism and other sensory challenges to stay focused. It enables users to limit the iOS device to stay on one application by disabling the Home button. You can even restrict touch input on certain parts of the screen.

Another feature that Apple has included is Safari Reader. This reduces visual distractions and clutter on a Web page so that users can focus on the content. These are just some of the built-in accessibility features that are included in Apple's mobile devices and mobile devices by companies such as Samsung and Google.

These features can be turned on by going to the Settings application. Once in Settings, users will need to click on *General* and select the *Accessibility* option. Users will see a list of accessibility features available on the device (figure 8.1). With these features enabled, librarians can assist users with disabilities in navigating resources or help them become more familiar with the technology, whether it is the user's personal device or one that the library lends.

This is just a partial list of ways that mobile devices can be used in libraries. Other possible uses include using tablets for displays or to replace desktop computers for specific tasks such as searching the catalog. Libraries can also use tablets for library instruction, and the list goes on—librarians just need to determine what works best for their library and its users.

◎ Mobile Solutions and Tools for Library Personnel

In addition to using mobile devices to create user-centered services, various applications for the use of mobile devices can aid library personnel as well. Mobile devices can be integrated for library personnel through open source software designed specifically for mobile devices; collaboration to create applications for data collection and reporting; roving reference services; and with a Web-based integrated library system.

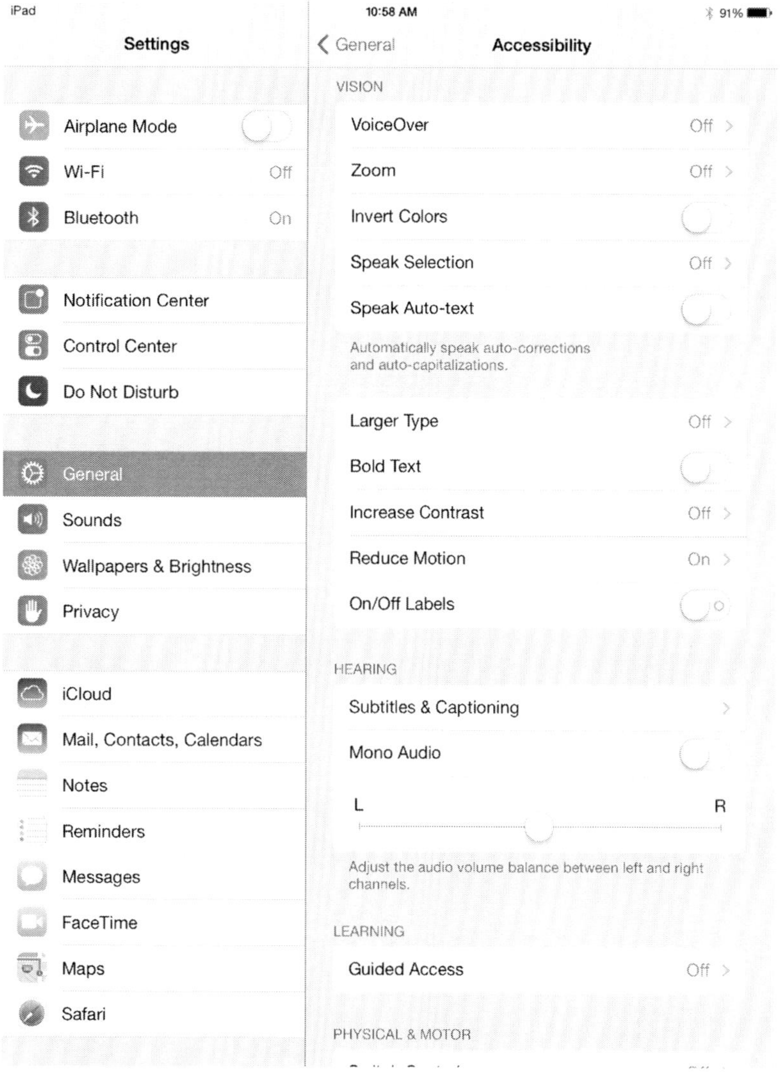

Figure 8.1. iPad accessibility features.

Open Source Software

Suma

Some libraries have focused on creating tools and applications for library personnel as a way to integrate mobile devices. Luckily for other libraries, some of that development has been released as open source software so that others can experiment with it without having to develop anything from the ground up. One library system that has done this is North Carolina State University Libraries. They created the Suma application. Suma is described as an open source mobile Web-based assessment toolkit for collecting and analyzing data about the usage of physical spaces and services in the library. Suma was designed and developed for use with tablets. The NCSU Libraries website states that the goals of Suma "include streamlining existing data collection, enabling fast, hassle-free mobile data collection, providing sophisticated data analysis and visualization capabilities for non-technical users, and promoting observational data analysis as an integral part of service and space design and day-to-day planning" (North Carolina State University Libraries 2013). The application is made up of three components that include data collection tools, a data management server, and a data reporting and analysis framework. The data reporting and analysis framework enables you to export the data in a variety of different formats, such as PNG images of charts, CSV export of raw data, and CSV export of summary statistics. NSCU Libraries have used Suma for:

- Building headcounts
- Service desk transactions
- Roaming reference services
- Experimental technology usage
- Media production activities
- Experimental space usage

The source code for Suma is freely available on GitHub, which is a Web-based hosting service for software projects that use the Git. Suma is a PHP-based application that needs to be installed on a Web server that has a MySQL database. So the installation requires the involvement of someone who has access to the server and knowledge of how to install a Web-based, database-backed application.

ShelfLister

For libraries that have the Voyager integrated library system, Michael Doran of the University of Texas at Arlington has developed open source software called ShelfLister. ShelfLister is a program that generates shelf lists. This program is useful for stacks maintenance, collection development, and inventory. The interface is designed for mobile devices. Two versions of the software are available; one is designed for smartphones (ShelfLister 2.0) and the other for tablets (ShelfLister 3.0).

The Ensor LRC at Georgetown College is one library that has used both versions of this open source program. Prior to implementation of ShelfLister, student workers would do inventory by shelf reading with a clipboard and a pen. Each student was assigned a certain range and would have to mark on the clipboard any items that were missing, damaged, or incorrectly shelved and any other issue. ShelfLister offered a better alternative for shelf reading and inventory. As a result, the Ensor LRC installed the program and purchased two iPods for use with ShelfLister 2.0 and later an iPad to use with ShelfLister 3.0.

To use ShelfLister, users need to enter a starting barcode and an ending barcode (LC call numbers can also be entered). Once the starting and ending barcodes are entered, a list of items is generated, either by call number or title, based upon what items should appear within the range of the barcodes entered. If an item is missing, damaged, misplaced, or falls under any other category listed, library personnel can mark it under the relevant category. Once an item is marked within a certain category, a text file is created on the Voyager server. Unfortunately, the program does not automatically update Voyager if an item is marked as missing, damaged, or under any other category. Once the text file is created, the information can then be put into a user-friendly format that can be used by the circulation staff to go in and manually update records. You can install ShelfLister fairly easily with just a few configurations. Although this is only available for libraries with Voyager, there may be similar programs available for other library systems.

Reference Stats

The Ensor LRC also started using iPads to collect reference desk statistics in the fall of 2013. With all the reference librarians equipped with iPads, the library began looking at ways for the librarians to use the devices for reference services. What developed from this was the idea to create a Web-based, database-backed application to collect reference statistics. Previously, statistics were tracked by marking transactions on a sheet of paper in a binder. The statistics would then have to be manually compiled at the end of the semester by the reference librarian, which took a considerable amount of time. Looking for a more efficient way to collect and tabulate reference statistics, librarians collaborated with the college's Information Technology Services to develop an application designed specifically for mobile devices that reference librarians could use to collect statistics and report them. As a result, the LRC Reference Stats website was developed (figure 8.2). The website allows the library to collect statistics for the following:

- Research questions
- Research appointments
- Online chats
- Phone calls
- Directional assistance
- Software assistance
- Printer issues

Additionally, the application allows librarians to add notes so others can see reoccurring questions that may be popping up. Librarians can undo a transaction if they have accidentally logged the wrong one. With the reporting mechanism, reference librarians can run a report without having to manually tabulate and can see what types of inquires the library is receiving at the reference desk. By looking at a way to integrate iPads into reference services, the librarians were able to transform the way they traditionally collected reference statistics.

Figure 8.2. Ensor LRC Reference Stats website.

Roving Reference

While it appears that more users are visiting libraries, some libraries are experiencing a decline in subject-related questions. Some reasons for this decline, especially in academic libraries, could be reluctance of students to leave their seat and lose access to a computer; fear that by approaching and seeking help at the desk, they are displaying their academic inadequacies to their fellow students; and other factors such as staff shortages and the advent of the Internet and wireless networks (Sharman and Walsh 2012). As a result, libraries have been seeking alternative ways to provide reference services to users. One way to do that is through roving reference services.

Roving reference is a service that extends beyond the traditional reference desk, with the goal of removing barriers between library personnel and library users. It can be used as a supplement to staffing the reference desk or as an alternative. The benefit of using tablets for this is that they allow library personnel to access resources without being tied to a computer at the reference desk.

There are several different approaches to roving reference. Some suggest that with roving reference, library personnel can move beyond the confines of the library to offer reference services. For an academic library, this might mean offering reference services at other places on campus, possibly the student center. Other approaches could be to keep the services within the library building and roam around the building to see if there are users that need assistance. There are many benefits no matter which approach is taken. Roving reference allows library personnel to reach and interact with users who may not approach the reference desk. It allows library staff to be more visible instead of being stuck behind a desk. Roving reference makes library personnel appear more accessible, and with tablets, more technologically accessible. It is also a way to approach library users more on their terms. Additionally, roving reference could be used to as a way to redefine library services as information literacy instruction. Using tablets enables librarians to download a variety of applications and create shortcuts to websites that allow them to access library resources quickly with the tap of an icon. Librarians can download the native applications provided by vendors and create shortcuts to access the library catalog and website.

Other ways that librarians can integrate mobile devices for use by personnel include library instruction, use with a Web-based integrated library system, and many more. As technology continues to expand, librarians will continue to look at ways not only to provide and extend services to library users but to make library personnel more available and useful as well.

Key Points

In addition to the various mobile solutions developed by libraries and provided by vendors, you can provide additional mobile services and solutions for both your users and your library personnel.

- Using mobile devices extends library services beyond websites and applications.
- Lending mobile devices to users enables access to mobile technology for more library users.
- Mobile devices can be valuable tools for library personnel.

- Mobile devices enable libraries to provide traditional services in new ways and in different formats.

After mobile services and projects have been initiated and completed, they need to be evaluated. This is the subject of the next chapter.

References

Hoffelder, N. 2013. "76% of US Libraries Offer eBooks, Nearly 2 in 5 Lend eReaders." *Digital Reader*, April 16. http://www.the-digital-reader.com/2013/04/16/76-of-us-libraries-offer-ebooks-nearly-2-in-5-lend-ereaders/#.UuaAcdIo6M9.

Hooksett Public Library. 2014. "eReaders for Loan at Your Library." http://www.hooksettlibrary.org/reading/ereaders-for-loan-at-your-library/.

L. E. Phillips Memorial Public Library. 2011. "@ Your Library—iPads!" https://ecpubliclibrary.info/services/library-services/ipads.html.

———. 2014. "iPad [catalog record]." http://www.more.lib.wi.us/search/o=690936270.

Luo, Lili. 2013. "Text a Librarian: Ideas for Best Practices." In *The Handheld Library: Mobile Technology and the Librarian*, edited by Thomas A. Peters and Lori Bell, 43–54. Santa Barbara, CA: Libraries Unlimited.

North Carolina State University Libraries. 2013. "Suma: A Mobile Space Assessment Toolkit." October 4. http://www.lib.ncsu.edu/dli/projects/spaceassesstool.

———. 2014. "Technology Lending." http://www.lib.ncsu.edu/techlending.

Oregon State University Libraries. 2014a. "Kindles." http://osulibrary.oregonstate.edu/kindle.

———. 2014b. "Tablets." http://osulibrary.oregonstate.edu/tablets.

River Falls Public Library. 2014. "Ebooks, Kindles and Library Digital Downloads Information." http://www.riverfallspubliclibrary.org/digital.html.

Sharman, Allison, and Andrew Walsh. 2012. "Roving Librarian at a Mid-Sized, UK-Based Library." *Library Technology Reports* 48, no. 8 (November/December): 28–34.

University of Louisville Libraries. 2013. "Kindles at Ekstrom and Kornhauser Health Sciences Libraries." http://louisville.libguides.com/Kindles.

CHAPTER 9

Evaluating and Maintaining Your Mobile Services and Resources

EVALUATION AND MAINTENANCE ARE IMPORTANT aspects of any projects, and mobile services and resources in libraries are no different. Even after a mobile initiative is implemented, libraries need to evaluate the initiative to determine how successful it has been and whether it has been worth the investment. Additionally, mobile services and resources need to be maintained as access to resources changes. The process is not over when a mobile service or resource has been implemented. In many ways, it has only just begun.

Evaluating Your Library's Mobile Services and Resources

Regardless of what type of mobile services and resources your library has decided to implement, there needs to be a process of evaluation to determine how successful those endeavors have been. Librarians can evaluate their mobile services and resources in a variety of different ways. How a library's mobile presence is evaluated will depend on the type of services and resources offered. For example, to track usage of a mobile website, you might use Google Analytics. Additionally, you might check to see how many times the library's native application has been downloaded. For libraries that lend mobile devices, circulation statistics might be an appropriate course of evaluation. Evaluation ensures that the resources being devoted to services are worth the investment of both time and money. A library incurs a significant financial cost if the decision is made to lend mobile devices to users, and a significant amount of time is required to develop and implement resources like mobile websites and native applications. Essentially, libraries need to determine whether patrons are using these mobile services and resources. An evaluation of mobile presence can enable libraries to see areas that need improvement, as well as areas that might need more focus. Let's take a look at some ways that you can evaluate your library's mobile presence.

Google Analytics

One way that you can evaluate your library's mobile presence is through the use of Google Analytics. Google Analytics is a service that generates detailed statistics about the traffic of a website as well as the sources that are used to access the website. This is a powerful tool that allows librarians, as well as other website administrators, to track a variety of different types of information about a library's online presence. Google Analytics features three important reporting mechanisms that provide a wealth of information for libraries. They are Audience, Acquisitions, and Behavior. Each of these reporting mechanisms contains an overview of the data available within each mechanism as well as additional reporting tools.

Audience

The tools in the Audience reporting mechanism are Demographics, Interests, Geo, Behavior, Technology, Mobile, Custom, and Visitors Flow. Of these tools, the Ensor Learning Resource Center at Georgetown College chose mainly to use just three: Behavior, Technology, and Mobile. The other reporting tools may hold some value to other libraries; however, they do not suit the needs of the Ensor Learning Resource Center. While the overview aspect of the Audience data allows you to see the number of website visits and page views, the specific reporting tools give a more detailed picture of how users are accessing the library's website and what devices they are using. The Behavior reporting tool allows you to see how many of your users are returning and how many new users are accessing the library website. You can also see the duration of visits to library Web pages in seconds. The Technology reporting tool allows you to see which browser (Internet Explorer, Chrome, FireFox, etc.) and which operating system users are accessing the library website with. The third Audience reporting function relating to mobile user behavior is the Mobile reporting tool. This reporting function allows you to see what category of device mobile users are accessing the website with. There are three device categories listed: desktop, mobile, and tablet. Additionally, you can see exactly what devices were used. For example, you can see how many times Apple iPhones, iPads, or Samsung Galaxy S4s were used to access the library's website or mobile website.

Acquisitions

The Acquisitions reporting mechanism gives you an overview of the different channels patrons are using to access your library's website. The most pertinent information can be found in the general overview. The data in the overview for Acquisitions lets you know whether users are coming to the library's website or mobile website directly. This reporting mechanism also lets libraries see other ways that users are accessing the library's online and mobile presence. You can see how many users are accessing through Organic Searches, which are natural search engine results that appear due to their relevance to the search terms. For example, someone might access the site by searching Google for "georgetown college library" or "ensor lrc." Additionally, you can see how users are being referred to your website. You can also see how many users are coming to the library's website from social media sites like Twitter and Facebook.

Behavior

The Behavior function allows you to see how many times users have visited the library's website. With this function, you can also see what Web pages are the most frequented among your user base. Additionally, options are available to see all the content contained in the library's website, along with data on how many times each Web page has been visited. The Behavior mechanism lets you see what the average load time for the website is. These three reporting mechanisms (Audience, Acquisitions, and Behavior) provide libraries with valuable data to evaluate their online and mobile Web presence.

In order to use this service, you will need to have a Google account. After you have created a Google account (or logged in with an existing one), you can add Google Analytics to your library's website and mobile website. To do that, you will need the JavaScript code that is generated to track your library's website usage. Once you have logged in to Google Analytics, click on the *Admin* link in the header of the page. You will then need to create a new account. Google will ask what you want to track. The two options will be *Website* and *Mobile App*. Select *Website*. You will then need to select a tracking method. The two options will be *Universal Analytics*, which is currently in Beta, and *Classic Analytics*. Choose *Classic Analytics*. Next you will need to provide an account name. For example, Ensor LRC is the account name for the Ensor Learning Resource Center. Then you will need to set up the property that you want to track. The name of the website and the URL will need to be provided. The property is the website where the code will be located. You can track multiple properties such as your library website, mobile website, and proxy login page under the same account. After you have completed these steps, click on *Get Tracking ID*. The next page contains your tracking ID, which will be something like this: UA-00000000-1. This is unique to the property that you want to track and will be different for each property that you decide to track. On this page, you will also find the JavaScript code that will need to go in the <head> tag of your library's website and mobile website. The JavaScript code will be similar to the following:

```
<script type="text/javascript">

var _gaq = _gaq || [];
_gaq.push(['_setAccount', 'UA-00000000-1']);
_gaq.push(['_trackPageview']);

(function() {
var ga = document.createElement('script'); ga.type =
'text/javascript'; ga.async = true;
```

```
ga.src = ('https:' == document.location.protocol ?
'https://ssl' : 'http://www') + '.google-analytics.com/
ga.js';
var s = document.getElementsByTagName('script')[0];
s.parentNode.insertBefore(ga, s);
})();
```

```
</script>
```

If your library uses a content management system like WordPress or Drupal, then this will need to be placed in the header.php file. If not, then this code will need to be added to each page that you want to track within this property.

In addition to being able to track website usage, Google Analytics also has some options available that enable libraries, as well as other developers, to track the usage of native applications. Google offers a service within Google Analytics called Mobile App Analytics that comes with its own software development kit (SDK). This is meant for developers that are working within the native environment using such programming languages as Java for Android and Objective-C for iOS. However, plugins for the PhoneGap framework allow developers to use Google Analytics. These plugins are available on GitHub.

Google Analytics is a powerful tool for libraries to measure how users are accessing their online presence, and with these plugins you can track the usage of native applications as well. Google Analytics can help you evaluate how much your library's mobile presence is being used. With this service, you can evaluate whether there needs to be a shift in focus. For example, if you see that more users are accessing the full library website with mobile devices and bypassing the mobile website, it might indicate that your library needs to consider developing a responsive website. Google Analytics is a tool that is specifically designed to track the usage of Web traffic; however, given that libraries are offering mobile services and resources through a variety of different ways, there are other methods that need to be used to evaluate services that are not Web based.

Circulation, Reference, and Vendor Statistics

As more and more libraries are lending mobile devices, they need to evaluate how effective the service is. In order to do that, libraries must rely on traditional means of collecting statistical data. What that means is looking at circulation statistics. Circulation statistics are often used to see what items are being checked out. While these statistics may not need to be as granular as seeing how many times each book in the library is checked out (although they can reach that level of detail), circulation statistics can show you what types of items are the most popular with your users. If your library is lending e-readers, tablets, or other mobile devices, circulation statistics can show how many times those devices have been checked out. By using circulation statistics, libraries can also get a glimpse of what user groups are frequently checking out certain items. In terms of e-readers, circulation statistics can help the library identify potential e-book titles to purchase and load on the devices.

Circulation statistics can be extremely useful when it comes to decision making. For libraries that decided to do a pilot project of lending mobile devices, circulation statistics can help determine whether the project was a success or if there is a more appropriate area in which to invest for mobile services and resources. Hold requests can also be useful for libraries lending mobile devices. If there are constant hold requests and mobile devices are always checked out, more devices might need to be purchased and circulated to meet the demands of your users. It also gives you a better idea of the types of devices, services, and resources your users are interacting with and expect to have access to through the library.

In addition to circulation statistics, you can also look at reference statistics to evaluate your mobile services and resources. Looking at reference statistics could be useful for libraries that offer the Text-a-Librarian service. Vendors like Mosio and LibraryH3lp provide this service to libraries with tiered plans on the amount of text messages a library can receive and send. Reference statistics can help libraries that offer this service by showing how often users are texting the library. It could aid you in deciding whether there is a need to increase your plan, leave it as is, lower it, or even discontinue the service. Both circulation and reference statistics can provide you with insights into your mobile services and resources that are not necessarily Web based and can aid in the decision-making process.

Aside from circulation and reference statistics, some library vendors such as EBSCO enable libraries to see how their mobile resources are being accessed. Libraries have little control over the development of resources from vendors; however, these often come with a subscription, and this can give you a glimpse into the research habits of your mobile users. To access statistics on mobile usage through EBSCO, you need to log in to your library's EBSCO*admin* account. Once you are logged in, click on *Standard Reports*. This will default to the tab Usage Reports. There are a few ways for libraries to get statistics on mobile usage from this point. One is to select the option *Browser and Device* under the Usage Reports tab. This report allows EBSCO*admin* administrators to retrieve usage data on specific Web browsers and mobile devices used to access EBSCO products through their library. The device part of this report will list the Hardware Vendor (Apple), Hardware Model (iPhone), OS/Platform (iOS), OS/Platform Version (iOS 7), Browser (Safari, Chrome for iOS, etc.), Browser Version, and Sessions. It will provide a grand total of sessions for both browsers and devices, though it does not break down the sessions that occurred specifically on mobile devices.

Another way to get mobile usage statistics from EBSCO is to select the *Interface* option. This option allows administrators to gather data on usage based on specific interfaces within EBSCO. With this report, you can view usage that comes through the mobile interface. To view these statistics, you will need to select the EBSCO*host* Mobile interface. Depending on the parameters selected, this report will display the number of sessions, searches, and total full-text requests, among other options, during a specific time frame.

However, not all vendors have the option for libraries to gather statistical data related to mobile usage. For vendors that do offer this option, you can use the information to gain insight into the potential research and searching habits of your mobile users. Although you do not have control over these mobile resources, statistical data on mobile usage provided by vendors can help you see what types of devices are being used to access your library's resources. It can also help you determine what types of mobile devices to target.

Circulation, reference, and vendor statistics are all useful tools you can use to evaluate library mobile services and resources. They are valuable for libraries that are lending mobile devices or offering a service like Text-a-Librarian, and they can help you gain insight into how often users are accessing resources provided by vendors through mobile devices.

Application Downloads

If you have developed native applications for specific mobile platforms such as iOS and Android, there is a way to evaluate your projects. You can track how many times your application or applications have been downloaded with developer tools provided by Apple and Google. You can use iTunes Connect for statistical data on iOS applications and Google Play for statistical data on Android applications. These tools should be familiar to library developers since they are the same mechanisms that are used to submit applications to the App Store and Google Play.

iTunes Connect

In addition to uploading an application for distribution on the App Store, iTunes Connect manages content sold on the App Store. With this tool, you can gather data on your library's iOS applications. To view application statistics, log in to iTunes Connect using your library's iOS Developer Account, and select *Sales and Trends*. On the next screen is a statistical overview for the previous week. The chart on this page will have two tabs, Units and Proceeds. The Units tab is for the number of units downloaded the previous week (this does not include updates, only new downloads). Proceeds contains information on the amount received from sales. Since most libraries release applications for free, this tab most likely will not be of any use.

Although the default is set to show you data from the previous week, you can also select one of the other options in iTunes Connect or use a custom date range to gather statistical data on downloads. The three other date options offered in iTunes Connect are Last 30 Days, Last Year, and Lifetime. The chart also lets you limit statistics by the following categories:

- Territory (location of user downloading the application)
- Platform (iPhone, iPad, or desktop)
- Category (category application is listed in on the App Store, e.g., education)
- Content type (iOS App)
- Transaction type (whether the application is free or paid for)

Additionally, you can download this data in CSV or XLS formats as well as export the content to the clipboard and paste it in a Word document.

Statistical data from iTunes Connect can show you how many times native iOS applications have been downloaded. This data can aid you in determining how successful developing native applications for iOS has been and whether to continue focusing on this mobile strategy or instead explore other avenues or platforms.

Google Play

If you have developed applications for the Android platform, Google Play can be used to gather statistical data for your library's Android applications. To view application statistics, log in to Google Play's Developers Console using the Google account associated with the developer profile. Once logged in, you will see an overview of applications that are listed in Google Play under your developer account. This screen gives an overview of the statistics for your library's applications. The data shown on this page include the App Name, Price, Current/Total Installs, Average Rating/Total Number of Ratings, Crashes & ANRs (Application Not Responding), Last Update, and Status. The Current/Total Installs is an area in which Google Play differs from iTunes Connect. In iTunes Connect, you can view how many times an application has been downloaded. In Google Play, you can see how many times an application has been downloaded (Total Installs) as well as the number of active devices that the application is currently installed on (Current Installs).

To get a more detailed report, click on the application. This page will display the product details and defaults to the Store Listing option. From here, click on *Statistics*. This page has more options to select from. The default view shows Current Installs by Device for the last month. Developers can select to see statistics for three months, six months, one year, or the entire time the application has been listed on Google Play. Additionally, the second chart on this page shows what version of Android a device is using. There are also options to see what Android devices the application is installed on, as well as the options for Country, Language, App Version, and Carrier. This constitutes one of several device statistical reports available. Overall, four different statistical reports are available for developers in the drop-down menu on the Statistics page; however, they are not categorized in the menu. The statistical categories are Device statistics, User statistics, Ratings statistics, and Crash and ANR Report statistics.

The Application Statistics Web page on the Android Developer's website gives a description of each statistical report available within each category. To get an in-depth description of what each statistical report is, look for the description under the Statistics heading and click on the *Learn More* link. Device statistics include current installs by device, daily installs by device, daily uninstalls by device, and daily upgraded by device. User statistics include the options current installs by user, total installs by user, daily installs by user, and daily uninstalls by user. Ratings statistics include daily average rating and cumulative average rating. The Crash and ANR Reports statistics include daily crashes and daily ANRs. In addition to these statistics, a heading at the bottom of each of the statistical report pages states "Get More Insights with Google Analytics for Mobile Apps." There are links to information on how to connect Google Analytics to the Developer Console and how to start using Google Mobile App Analytics.

The methods listed here are just some of the tools you can use to evaluate your library's mobile services and resources. They are by no means the only ways to do so. An additional way to evaluate your library's mobile presence is getting feedback from users regarding the mobile services and resources available to them. Regardless of the means used to evaluate these services and resources, it is an important process. In addition to the evaluation of mobile services and resources, it's important to make sure your library is maintaining its current mobile process so that users have access to the most up-to-date services and resources.

Maintaining Your Library's Mobile Services and Resources

Now that your library has decided to create and develop a mobile presence, those services and resources need to be maintained. The type of mobile presence that your library has decided to undertake will determine the process by which you maintain those mobile services and resources. In fact, the maintenance for each facet of your mobile presence will vary. This section offers some insight into ways to maintain your library's mobile services and resources.

Updating the Library's Mobile or Responsive Website

The library website is an evolving resource that needs to be maintained and updated as access to resources changes and organizational changes occur. The same is also true of the library's mobile Web presence; whether it's a mobile website or a responsive website, services and resources need to be continuously updated so that users have access to the most recent information. If your library has a separate mobile website, both the traditional website and the mobile website will need to be updated. On the other hand, if your library has developed a responsive website, then the services and resources need only be updated once. Some of the tasks of updating the library's mobile Web presence might have to be done manually. These might include changes to library hours, library personnel listings, and resource links. If your library uses a content mangement system (CMS) like WordPress, then you will be notified if any link on your website is broken instead of having to manually check each link.

In addition to updating the services and resources, as new versions of mobile frameworks or responsive frameworks are released, your library may want to see what additional features could be added to enhance the mobile experience. For example, the jQuery Mobile framework is constantly improving and adding new features. One feature that did not exist in earlier iterations of the software was the option to add panels. Panels in jQuery Mobile are designed as flexible tools to allow for the easy creation of menus and other elements. You could use this feature in your library's mobile website to create menus and enhance navigation on mobile devices. This is just one example. As mobile technology continues to expand, so will the way your library provides online access, especially mobile access, to services and resources.

Updating Mobile Devices

Libraries that lend mobile devices to their users also need to update and maintain those devices. Various tasks must be completed to update and maintain a mobile device lending program. These tasks will vary depending on what devices a library is lending.

If your library lends e-readers like the Kindle, new titles need to be added to the devices. What this means is that e-reader devices need to be synced to the library's account to reflect the current list of titles available. New titles can be added through suggestions from library personnel or users. In addition to adding new titles, every time an e-reader is returned, the device must be inspected for damage and any content that users may have downloaded or erased. For example, if your library deregisters Kindle devices before they are checked out, users can register those devices to their accounts and purchase content. That content needs to be erased and the device deregistered again before it can be checked out by another patron. However, some libraries may restrict users from downloading any additional content onto e-readers. Libraries handle the circulation of e-readers differently, but regardless of the policies, these devices need to be evaluated every time they come back in, and the devices need to be synced to the library's account to ensure that newly purchased titles have been added.

If your library lends mobile devices like tablets, a variety of other considerations go into maintaining and updating the device. While new titles do not need to be added to a tablet, applications do. At the outset of the lending process, libraries identify the applications to load onto the tablet for users to have access to. As more and more applications become available, you will need to stay aware of what is being developed and released and which programs might benefit your users. This will require library personnel interacting with and testing new applications for consideration. New applications may also be suggested by users. This could be similar to patron-driven acquisitions for mobile devices. You will also to need to erase any downloaded content added by users. The device may need to be reset to the factory settings and the library's profile added, or the device might need to be reimaged.

With tablets and other mobile devices, you need to be aware of available software updates. Software updates for mobile devices could add additional features, or come with minor and/or major bug fixes. Updating the software can improve the user experience but may also affect certain installed applications. In addition to software updates, applications installed on mobile devices will need to be routinely updated to ensure that users have access to the most recent version. Luckily for libraries, as well as other consumers, some mobile platforms enable application updates to be turned on automatically, so when a new update is available it is immediately installed on the device.

Updating the Library's Native Applications

Just as resources need to be updated on the library's website and mobile website as they change, the same goes for the native applications developed for the library. As resources change, library staff depart or arrive, and library hours change (among other things), native applications need to be updated to reflect these changes. Additionally, once you have developed a native application for your library, you may also want to consider extending the functionality of the application to take advantage of new or advanced features available on mobile devices.

To update your library's application, open the project in Xcode, if you developed an iOS application, or Eclipse, if you developed an application for Android. Updating services, resources, and personnel are similar to updating a responsive or mobile website if the PhoneGap framework was used. If this is the case, navigate to the www folder in the project and select the HTML file that needs to be updated. Once the file or files are updated, you are ready to resubmit the application to the App Store or Google Play. If you wish to add additional functionality and take advantage of some of the advanced features of mobile devices, there are a variety of plugins available for PhoneGap.

Starting with version 3.0, Cordova, the underlying software of PhoneGap, implements all mobile device application programming interfaces (APIs) as plugins, and these are disabled by default. Plugins are pieces of add-on code that provide access to the native components of a device. Some are built within the framework (Camera, Device Motion, FileTransfer, and others), while additional plugins are created by developers. There are two different ways to install plugins into a PhoneGap project. The first is by using the command-line interface (CLI) that was installed and used to set up the PhoneGap project. To install a plugin using this method, open the command prompt program. To add the Camera plugin, run the following command:

```
cordova plugin add org.apache.cordova.camera
```

To add a plugin that was created by an external developer—for example, a social sharing plugin—you will need to run the following command, replacing org.apache.cordova. camera with the link to the new plugin:

```
cordova plugin add https://github.com/mgcrea/cordova-face-
book-connect.git
```

Instead of specifying the location of the plugin with the framework, you will provide a link to the plugin. PhoneGap's website, as well as the GitHub website, contains additional documentation on how to further configure individual plugins for your application.

The second way to install plugins for your PhoneGap project is to use a lower-level Plugman command-line interface. This type of installation is called native platform development workflow (PhoneGap 2014). The difference between the two methods is that the CLI can install plugins for all platforms you are targeting, while Plugman can only install the plugin on one platform at a time. Before you can use this method, Plugman needs to be installed. To install it, open the command prompt and run the following command:

```
npm install -g plugman
```

Node.js needs to be installed on your computer to install Plugman. Since this is the way that PhoneGap was installed, this should not be an issue. Now that this command-line interface has been installed, you can use it to install plugins for your project. To install a plugin—for example, the Camera plugin for iOS—open the command prompt and run the following command:

```
plugman --platform ios --project LibraryApp --plugin org.
apache.cordova.camera
```

To install plugins from external developers, add the link to the plugin in place of org. apache.cordova.camera. These are two examples of how you can install plugins to add additional functionality and take advantage of the native components of mobile devices. Once you are done updating and adding any additional functionality to your application, you are ready to submit an update of your library's application to the App Store or Google Play.

Submitting an Update to the App Store

Now that you have updated the application in Xcode, it is time to submit it to the App Store. To submit an update, go to iTunes Connect and click on *Manage Your Apps*. Select the application that you want to update. On this screen, you will see two sections, App Information and Versions. Under the Versions section, you will see the current version of your library's iOS application with details about the status, when it was created, and when it was released. There will also be an option to add a new version of the application. This option needs to be selected to add the updated application to the App Store. Click on *Add Version*. On the next screen, you need to provide the version of the application as well as what is different in the new version that you are uploading. After you have entered in the information, click *Save*. At this point, if there are any requirements that need to be updated in iTunes Connect (e.g., icons and screenshots), you will get a message to update them before proceeding. If nothing needs to be added, the status of the application will change to *Prepare for Upload* and the option *Ready to Upload Binary* will appear in the top right corner of the screen. Now that you have completed the setup to add a new version of your library's iOS application, it is time to head back over to Xcode to create the archive and upload the binary file.

Adding a new version of the application is similar to submitting the first version, except there are three additional options in iTunes Connect. One option that you should have already completed is What's New in This Version. The second option is Version Release Control, which is where you can set the date that the new version will be released, pending App Store approval, or you can elect to have the new version of the application released automatically after it is approved. The third additional option is iCloud Availability. More than likely this will not affect library applications, but if you are updating an iOS application for legal or usability reasons, you can elect not to have the previous version of the application available on iCloud.

To submit a new version of the application, follow the same steps as when the application was first submitted to the App Store. Since this will be a new version of the library's application, you will need to change the version number. To do that, select your project in the left pane. Next, click on the project name under Targets. In the General tab, find Version in the Identity section and change the version of the application. Now an archive needs to be created. Make sure that an iOS device is connected and that the scheme in Xcode is set to an iOS device, not the simulator. In the menu bar at the top of the screen, select *Product*. Once the menu is open, select *Archive*. The Organizer in Xcode Organizer should automatically open and list the archive that was just created. On this screen there will be two options, Validate and Distribute. Choose *Validate*. This will send the new version of the application through a process to check that all needed elements are packaged with the application. If the new version passes validation, it is ready to distribute to the App Store and go through Apple's approval process. If it fails, there will be an error message listing the issues. Once those are fixed in Xcode, create another archive and repeat the validation process. After the validation process is complete, click *Distribute* and follow the directions on the subsequent screens to submit the new version of the application for approval.

After the submission process is successful, the next step is to wait for the review process. The status of the application on iTunes Connect will change to *Waiting for Review*. This completes the process of submitting a new version of your library's application to the App Store. When it is available on the App Store to download, the status on iTunes Connect will change to *Ready for Sale*. That is the process for submitting an update of your library's application to the App Store.

Submitting an Update to Google Play

The process to submit an update to your library's Android application does not follow the same submission process as iOS applications do. The process for exporting the Android application package (APK) file from Eclipse is the same, but updating the application in Google Play is different. Once you have made the changes to the library's Android application, you need to make sure that the version of the application is changed. If not, then you will get an error when the APK file is uploaded to Google Play. To change the version of the application before it is exported from Eclipse, locate the XML file named AndroidManifest. At the very top of this file will be the following markup:

```
<?xml version="1.0" encoding="utf-8"?>
<manifest xmlns:android="http://schemas.android.com/apk/
res/android"
package="com.benrawlins.LibraryApp"
android:versionCode="1"
android:versionName="1.0">
<application android:icon="@drawable/icon" android:
label="@string/app_name">
```

```
. . .
</application>
</manifest>
```

This is where the version of the application will need to be changed before it is exported. The android:versionCode and android:versionName will need to be changed, but they do not have to be the same. For example, the android:versionCode might be "2," which means that this is the second iteration of the application, while the android:versionName might be "1.01." The android:versionName is the version that will be displayed to users on Google Play. Once the version is changed, you can export the application and prepare to submit the APK file to Google Play.

To upload the new APK file to Google Play, log in to the Developer Console. Once logged in, you will see a listing of the applications in your account. If your library has developed more than one application, select the one that you are updating. Once you have selected the application that you wish to update, you will be taken to a screen with the Store Listing. To upload the new APK file, select the APK option in the navigation bar on the left. On this page, there will be an option to *Upload new APK to Production*. Click on this and navigate to where the new APK file is stored on your computer and upload it to Google Play. Once the new APK file is uploaded, choose the option *Publish now to Production* to release the new version of your Android application. Once this step is completed, navigate back to the Store Listing. In the Store Listing, you will need to add a description of what changes have been made to the new version. To do that, find where it says "Recent changes" and add the changes that you have made. Once the new version of the application is published, it should be available on Google Play within a very short amount of time, typically no longer than an hour or two.

Beyond the Library

Successful mobile projects, like the development of mobile websites and native applications, can lead to libraries looking at ways to expand their mobile presence. This is being done by the development of historical walking tours designed specifically for mobile devices, most notably by academic libraries. Libraries that have undertaken such a mobile project are the North Carolina State University Libraries (WolfWalk), Oregon State University Libraries (BeaverTracks), Ohio State University Libraries (Buckeye Stroll), and the Ensor Learning Resource Center at Georgetown College (TigerTrax). These mobile projects extend the library's mobile presence beyond traditional library services and resources. They can also serve as valuable marketing tools; more on that in the next chapter.

⊚ Key Points

There are a variety of different ways that you can evaluate mobile services and resources, as well as maintain and update them.

- Libraries can use a service like Google Analytics for statistics on the usage of mobile websites and even native applications.
- Plugins for PhoneGap can be used to add additional functionality to library applications.

- The library's mobile presence needs to be updated to reflect changes in services and resources.
- The processes to submit updates of your library applications to the App Store and Google Play follow many of the same steps as submitting the initial applications.

Now that your library has made an investment in mobile services and resources, it is important to get the word out to your users. The next chapter will focus on marketing your library's mobile services and resources.

Reference

PhoneGap. 2014. "Using Plugman to Manage Plugins." PhoneGap Documentation. http://docs .phonegap.com/en/3.4.0/plugin_ref_plugman.md.html#Using%20Plugman%20to%20 Manage%20Plugins.

CHAPTER 10

Marketing Your Library's Mobile Services and Resources

MARKETING IS A WAY TO MAKE USERS AWARE of services and resources. It is an essential component of any organization, and all institutions, no matter how small or large their effort might be, participate in marketing. Libraries are no different. Libraries offer a wealth of information and services that users may not be aware of. Marketing provides an opportunity to promote services and resources to users so that they have a full grasp of what is offered at their library. Given that your library has invested effort, time, and money in offering mobile resources and services, it is essential that your users be made aware of them. Marketing provides the avenue to do just that.

Principles of Marketing and Libraries

Before you and your library can effectively market your mobile services and resources (or any services and resources for that matter), it is important to have a basic understanding of the fundamental principles of marketing. Philip Kotler is one of the foremost authorities on marketing, and an examination of the marketing principles that he developed will be useful for your library. He defines marketing as

> the science and art of exploring, creating, and delivering value to satisfy needs of a target market at a profit. Marketing identifies unfilled needs and desires. It defines, measures, and quantifies the size of the identified market and the profit potential. It pinpoints which segments the company is capable of serving best and it designs and promotes appropriate products and services. (Kotler 2012)

He also identifies several key processes of marketing. They are opportunity identification, new product development, customer satisfaction, customer retention and loyalty building, and order fulfillment (Kotler 2012). Many business experts point out that companies that are able to handle these processes well tend to be successful, and those that don't will not survive.

These key processes of marketing can also be applied to libraries. Libraries are continuously looking for new and innovative ways to actively engage with users, and one opportunity that has become vital, if not essential, is mobile technology. As a result, libraries are developing mobile services and resources (our products) to reach the growing mobile user base. Customer satisfaction is a top priority for libraries, as it's important to make sure that users are satisfied with the services and resources that are being provided. Customer satisfaction helps libraries, as well as other institutions and organizations, build loyal users and customers. With libraries competing with the likes of Google and other companies for information access, building a loyal user base is essential, and providing access to mobile-optimized content and services can certainly help that cause. Libraries may not fill orders in the sense that other institutions or organizations do (although interlibrary loan could be an example), but users engage with services and resources at libraries to fulfill their need for information.

Philip Kotler has also established the four Ps of the marketing mix, which many consider the gospel of marketing. The four Ps of marketing are product, price, place, and promotion. These four elements are variables to help businesses create a strategy to market products and services to targeted consumers. Let's take a look at each of the four Ps and see how they apply to libraries and the services and resources they offer—especially mobile services and resources.

Product

A product is the good or service a business offers to consumers. In addition to the physical product itself, there may be other attributes or elements that attract consumers to products, including features, options, services, warranties, and the brand (Ehmke, Fulton, and Lusk 2005). Some questions companies consider in the product aspect of their marketing mix are:

- What does the consumer want from the product or service?
- What needs does it satisfy?
- What features of the product meet these needs?
- How and where will the customer use it?
- What should the name of the product or service be?
- How will it be branded? (Mind Tools 2014)

The library product that you are trying to market to your users is a mobile service or resource. It could be a mobile website or native application that was developed by your library, or a service like Text-a-Librarian. Regardless of what mobile resource or service you are trying to market, you will be faced with many of these same questions. For example, you may need to determine what users want from the service or resource, or whether it fulfills a need for your users, along with other questions.

Price

Price is the amount a business charges for their products and services. Questions that companies might consider include:

- What is the value of the product or service to consumers?
- Is the consumer price sensitive?
- Will a small decrease in price gain us extra market share? (Mind Tools 2014)

Price is the least relevant of the four Ps because many of the services provided by libraries do not cost users anything. This goes for mobile services and resources as well. Whether libraries are providing a mobile-based service, like Text-a-Librarian, or developing mobile applications, those services and resources are offered at no cost to users. However, while there may not be a price for users, the price to provide mobile services and resources is a main consideration for libraries. Libraries need to evaluate the price, whether it be in money or resources allocated, to determine if the benefits to users outweigh the costs.

Place

Place refers to the distribution channels that businesses use to get their products on the market. Possible questions that companies might consider include:

- Where do buyers look for our product or service?
- If they look in a store, what kind? A specialist boutique or a supermarket, or both? Or online? Or direct, via a catalogue?
- How can we access the right distribution channels? (Mind Tools 2014)

Identifying the right distribution channels is an important aspect of the marketing mix. For libraries, places and avenues need to be identified to alert users of the various mobile services and resources available. The distribution channels for mobile library services and resources are through the use of mobile technology.

Promotion

The fourth piece of the marketing mix is promotion. Promotion is when a company begins to think of ways to advertise and promote their product and service. The purpose of promotion is to give consumers an idea of what your product is, what it can be used for, and why they need to purchase it. Apple cofounder Steve Jobs once said that "a lot of times, people don't know what they want until you show it to them" (Mui 2011). Promotion allows companies to showcase products to consumers who may be unaware that the product exists or of its capabilities and benefits. In essence, promotion is a way to show consumers what they want. Companies consider the following questions when developing a plan to promote a product or service:

- Where and when can we get across our marketing messages to our target market?
- Will we reach our audience by advertising in the press, or on TV, or on radio, or on billboards? By using direct-marketing mail? Through PR? On the Internet?
- When is the best time to promote? (Mind Tools 2014)

One of the important questions that companies need to consider is what formats they will use to promote their product or service. This aspect of the marketing mix is the one that libraries tend to focus on the most. For libraries, promotion is a way that they can make their users aware of the mobile services and resources available at the library. There are a variety of different formats to consider when promoting any type of service or resource, and choosing the right ones is essential.

These are the elements that make up the marketing mix that many institutions and organizations adhere to, along with some variations, to engage their users. Now that you have an understanding of the principles of marketing and how they relate to libraries, it is time to look at some ways that you can market your mobile services and resources to your users.

Marketing Mobile Library Services and Resources

Marketing in libraries is often a tricky business. Like many other nonprofit institutions, most libraries do not have a dedicated marketing department. Ned Potter, author of *The Library Marketing Toolkit*, explains the issues with marketing in libraries:

> Marketing is normally low on the list of priorities (we're happy to spend X millions acquiring resources, but only X hundred on telling people why they might want to use them) and library promotion is most often done by people who already had a full time job within the organization before they were asked to start. (Grant 2013)

Potter also states that marketing for libraries is tough for all sorts of reasons. Some of those include lack of time, lack of funding, as well as lack of resources. Regardless of the difficulties of marketing, it is an important task that libraries need to be concerned with.

To demonstrate how essential marketing is for libraries, consider the example of e-books. Although e-books are not exclusively accessible on mobile devices, many people use their mobile devices to read and access e-books. Despite this, many users are unaware that their library lends e-books and are even more uncertain of how to access them on their devices. The Pew Research Center found that in 2012 only 12 percent of Americans aged sixteen and older reported borrowing an e-book from their local library. Even more telling is that 62 percent said they were not aware that they could borrow e-books from their local public library. At the time, more than 75 percent of public libraries in the United States were lending e-books (Pew Internet and American Life Project 2012). The problem is not that interest in and access to e-books is lacking; it is that many users are unaware that free e-books are available at their local library. The Pew Research Center found that:

- 58 percent of all library card holders say they do not know if their library provides e-book lending services.

- 55 percent of all those who say the library is "very important" to them say they do not know if their library lends e-books.
- 53 percent of all tablet computer owners say they do not know if their library lends e-books.
- 48 percent of all owners of e-book reading devices such as original Kindles and NOOKs say they do not know if their library lends e-books.
- 47 percent of all those who read an e-book in the past year say they do not know if their library lends e-books. (Pew Internet and American Life Project 2012)

These findings exemplify the importance of marketing in libraries, and especially marketing mobile resources to users who have mobile devices. If our users are unaware of the mobile resources they can access, they are not going to use them. Marketing gives libraries the opportunity to ensure that users are aware of the vast services and resources, including mobile, that are available to them.

One thing that is essential when marketing any service or resource at your library is to develop a marketing plan. In developing a marketing plan, you and your library need to focus on what you hope to achieve. Ned Potter (2013) points out that there is often a fundamental misunderstanding in libraries of what marketing should actually achieve. Focusing on your expectations from the marketing plan can yield better results than having no expectations or understanding of what your library hopes to achieve. Libraries often run small marketing efforts using e-mails or flyers (and sometimes both) to promote events, services, or resources, but the results of these small efforts are less than ideal. Potter explains that we need to think about how much it takes for us as consumers to take action. Was it one small promotion that led a consumer to purchase a product or service? Often not. He states that instead of these "one-off" promotions, libraries should consider strategic marketing (Potter 2013). Strategic marketing is a series of related campaigns over a period of time that can yield better results than what appear to be different unrelated events and promotions.

A marketing plan can help your library effectively promote your mobile services and resources, as well as other services and resources available at your library. The ways you market your mobile services and resources may, in most ways, be similar to how you market your library's other services and resources. A variety of different online examples and templates for developing a library marketing plan can be adapted and applied specifically to marketing mobile services and resources. The New Mexico State Library has a Library Marketing Plan Workbook that explains the importance of marketing for libraries. The Library Marketing Plan Workbook outlines seven steps for developing a library marketing plan. They are as follows:

- Step one is to understand your community and what they want (not what they need).
- Step two is to understand your users.
- Step three is picking a niche.
- Step four is developing your library's marketing message.
- Step five is determining your marketing mediums.
- Step six is setting marketing goals that are SMART (sensible, measurable, achievable, realistic, and time specific).
- Step seven is developing your marketing budget to execute the plan. (New Mexico State Library 2014)

This template gives libraries a basic blueprint for developing a marketing plan and is general enough that it can be applied specifically to mobile library services and resources.

Another good example is the 2013–2015 Rutgers University Libraries Marketing Plan. In their plan, Rutgers University Libraries created broad overall goals that they hope to achieve as well as supporting goals. The two overall goals are:

- To raise the visibility of the Rutgers University Libraries among undergraduates, graduate students, faculty, staff, alumni, and other audiences as appropriate
- To support the priorities of the Rutgers University Libraries Strategic Plan, 2012–2015 (Rutgers University Libraries 2012)

In addition to the overall goals, Rutgers University Libraries created four supporting goals. Each of these supports one of the overall goals and gives suggested actions and measures. An example of a supporting goal from their marketing plan is shown in textbox 10.1.

While the focus of these samples is not solely on marketing mobile services and resources, they provide examples of well-thought-out library marketing plans that have defined goals and expectations. They are both good models to use in developing a marketing plan for your library's mobile services and resources. However, rather than develop a marketing plan solely for mobile services and resources, you may want to include your mobile objectives within an overall library marketing plan. For example, you could include a goal in

TEXTBOX 10.1.

2013–2015 RUTGERS UNIVERSITY LIBRARIES MARKETING PLAN

Supporting Goal #3: Become a visible partner in all appropriate Rutgers major events, on all campuses, such as Rutgers Day, Scarlet Knight Days, TA orientations, alumni reunion weekend, international student orientation, new faculty orientation, and prospective student tours. This supporting goal is intended to support priority #4 in the Libraries Strategic Plan.

Suggested Actions

- Identify and prepare giveaway items that are appropriate for the functions to be attended
- Arrange for Libraries representation at select functions as identified and track number of table visitors, types of questions asked, and response to giveaway items

Suggested Measures

- Successful staffing of target events
- Number of visitors per event
- Consumption of giveaways
- (When possible to collect) list of questions asked most frequently (Rutgers University Libraries 2012)

your plan to increase awareness of the mobile services and resources available at your library and define ways that your library could achieve that goal. Once your library has created a marketing plan that includes mobile services and resources and sets expectations, you can turn your attention to the various ways to promote these resources available to your library.

Library Website

A good place to start marketing mobile services and resources is with your library's website. Library websites are packed with a lot of information and are the source most users will access to find information regarding library services and resources, making it a valuable marketing tool for your mobile services.

You can promote your mobile services on your library website in several ways. A slideshow or announcement on the home page of the library website is a good way to promote a particular mobile service or resource. You can then link the slide or announcement to another page on your website that gives users more detailed information about how to use the mobile-based service or access the mobile-optimized resource.

Another way to promote and increase awareness of your library's mobile services and resources is by creating visible links to them on your website, preferably on the home page. If there are no visible links to mobile services and resources, users will assume there are no mobile options available to them. If you have a mobile library website, ensure that there is some kind of indicator, either a link or a linked image, letting users access it from your full website. A good example of this is the Michigan State University Libraries. On the home page of their website, there are several icons; one of these icons is a mobile phone that links to the mobile website. The phone icon is in line with other icons linking users to various social media accounts, and these are clearly visible to users who visit the library's website. If your library has developed a native application, or had one developed by a third-party vendor like Boopsie, make sure that a link or links to the app stores are visible so users can download it.

Additionally, the library website is a good place to promote mobile websites and applications available from vendors. With more and more vendors offering mobile-optimized access to resources, it is important that users are aware of these mobile research options. To promote these materials, you could create a mobile resources Web page that outlines all the resources available in a mobile-optimized format. Wheaton College in Massachusetts has a link to Mobile Research on the home page of the library's website. Once users click on the link, they see a listing with details of all the mobile-optimized resources available for their information needs. Many other libraries have taken this approach or have created LibGuides (more on that in a moment) to promote the mobile services and resources available at their library.

Since most library users will be accessing the library website as a path to fulfill their need for information, it is an essential to help spread the word about mobile services and resources available to them. Promoting mobile services and resources on your library website does not require anything especially fancy, although a nicely designed slide, banner, or button would be beneficial.

LibGuides

Many libraries are using LibGuides as a way to showcase mobile resources as well as useful mobile-optimized resources that users might find helpful. Creating a LibGuide to market and promote mobile services and resources enables your users to see the variety of options that are available to them. These options could include mobile-based services, resources developed by the library, and mobile-optimized options available from library vendors. In the case of native applications, a LibGuide can inform users what platform certain resources are available on. The creation of a LibGuide to showcase and promote mobile services and resources also serves to promote the knowledge of the library staff about useful mobile technology. The University of California San Francisco, Baylor University Libraries, and Columbus State Community College are examples of libraries that have created a LibGuide for mobile resources to ensure that their users are aware of the wide array of mobile options available.

LibGuides can be a useful tool in providing mobile users with detailed instructions on how to access certain resources. For example, users may want to access EBSCO eBooks on their mobile device but may not know how to download them. The Ensor Learning Resource Center has created a LibGuide promoting the EBSCO eBook collections available at the library, as well as detailed instructions on downloading. While some vendors offer mobile-optimized options to access content on users' mobile devices, some resources require the use of a third-party native application. EBSCO eBooks is one of those resources. The LibGuide instructs users to download the third-party application Bluefire Reader, which is built on the Adobe digital publishing platform. Once the application is downloaded and authorized using their Adobe ID, users can download and check out EBSCO eBooks on their personal mobile device. LibGuides provide you with opportunities to promote the mobile services and resources available at your library, as well as increase the knowledge of your library staff regarding mobile technology.

Social Media

An additional online medium that libraries can use to market and promote their mobile services and resources is social media. According to the Pew Research Center, 73 percent of online adults use social media sites (Pew Internet and American Life Project 2013). Further, 60 percent of the time spent on social media sites comes from mobile devices. While these numbers may not be too surprising, they do signify that social media offers an excellent and exciting opportunity to market mobile library services and resources. Marketing on social media can help reach a potentially larger audience and allows users to share or like content, enabling their social media friends to see the content that they have shared or liked. Social media can, in some ways, be seen as digital word of mouth.

The strategy for marketing on social media will vary depending on which platform(s) you choose. For example, Twitter has a limitation of 140 characters per tweet, and Instagram is a photo-sharing site. However, most social media sites are focused on mobile users and have developed native applications for a broad range of platforms.

Despite this, some libraries have a difficult time engaging their users through social media. Nancy Dowd says, if that is the case, then your library is probably posting the wrong things or not understanding your audience (Dowd 2013). With social media, libraries are competing with all kinds of different posts. On Facebook, for example, to help your library stand out, Ben Bizzle, director of technology for Crowley Ridge Regional Library, says,

> Make them laugh and pull their heart strings. Facebook gives you a tiny little space that is competing with hundreds of other posts. You will never be able to convey anything with

any depth or detail, so don't try. But you can use that space as a way to entice people to click on a link to learn more or sign up for a cool program. (Dowd 2013)

With the various social media outlets available, libraries are becoming more and more aware of their usefulness to promote services and resources. Take Pinterest, for example. Pinterest is a pinboard-style, photo-sharing website that allows users to create and manage theme-based image collections such as events, interests, and hobbies. The American Library Association points out that libraries are generally using Pinterest to promote services and resources. Examples include:

- Pinning book covers. Many librarians use the visual power of Pinterest to display book covers, especially those from new books, special collections, and child-friendly material.
- Creating reading lists on a wide range of topics.
- Getting the word out on recent acquisitions.
- Fostering research. Much Pinterest material is on the light side, but some librarians and academics see potential in the site for much more serious applications.
- Promoting library activities, showcasing everything from lectures to job help and author visits.
- Offering access to digital collections. With e-books gaining in popularity, some libraries are using Pinterest to share links to new digital materials. (American Library Association 2013)

There are a variety of different ways to effectively market library services and resources on social media platforms. Take, for example, Ann Handley's tips for posting on social media sites shown in textbox 10.2.

Many libraries are using social media platforms to market services and resources to users. In a presentation regarding the use of social media at Brooklyn College Library, Deimosa Webber-Bey and Miriam Deutch provided some best practices for libraries using different social media platforms. While the presentation focused specifically on

TEXTBOX 10.2.

TIPS FOR POSTING ON SOCIAL MEDIA

- Keep the goal of your post top of mind—*why* are you posting this?
- Write compelling headlines—precise and/or funny.
- Lead with the good stuff—give a solid overview in first phrase.
- Make every word count—do *not* abbreviate.
- Keep it simple—less is more; link to the full story.
- Provide context—use keywords and hashtags.
- Graphics expand the story—visually describe your headline; scan an image or take a picture if necessary.
- People make things interesting—use a conversational tone.
- Consider the reader—respect your audience and think twice before you post. (CUNY Academic Commons 2014)

social media in academic libraries, many of their suggestions can be applied to all types of libraries (see textboxes 10.3, 10.4, and 10.5 for their best practices suggestions). These are ways that you can use various social media platforms to market library services and resources, particularly those that are mobile. However, you need to choose the platforms that you believe will actively engage your users.

TEXTBOX 10.3.

BEST PRACTICES FOR FACEBOOK

- Share images from the library's special collections that relate to current events.
- Post flyers for library events.
- Link to resources, especially library-made ones.
- Promote library services, particularly digital tools. (Webber-Bey and Deutch 2013)

TEXTBOX 10.4.

BEST PRACTICES FOR TWITTER

- Tweet archival images of students on campus, particularly in the library on #throwbackthursday.
- Promote publications and presentations by librarians.
- Respond to directional questions.
- Respond to criticism of the library facilities or services promptly. (Webber-Bey and Deutch 2013)

TEXTBOX 10.5.

BEST PRACTICES FOR INSTAGRAM

- Post unique and interesting pictures of students in the stacks.
- Post archival photos of students on campus, particularly in the library, for #throwbackthursday.
- Advertise and hold photo contests.
- Share pictures of new furniture, hardware, and artwork at the library. (Webber-Bey and Deutch 2013)

Library Instruction

In addition to the online tools available to market and promote mobile services and resources, librarians need to take advantage of marketing opportunities that do not exist online. One way to do that is through library instruction. Library instruction is not something that is generally thought of as a marketing tool. While the goal of library instruction is to assist your users in finding, evaluating, and using information effectively, in doing so you are promoting the services and resources available at your library. Additionally, library instruction provides you with the opportunity to demonstrate the services and resources available to your users.

A library instruction session is an opportune time to promote your library's mobile services and resources as well. If you are demonstrating to your users how to use a particular database that is also mobile optimized, you can inform them that if they have a smartphone or other type of mobile device, they can search that particular database as well. For example, you may mention that EBSCO has a mobile website interface and mobile applications for the iOS and Android platforms. If you have a text-a-call-number feature in the library catalog, demonstrate that feature to your users when you are showing them how to search and find materials using the catalog. If users do not know how to use and interact with the mobile services and resources that are available, then they will be neglected by your mobile users.

Offering a workshop on mobile technology available at your library is another form of instruction you can use to market and promote your mobile services and resources. Workshops allow you to demonstrate services and resources to users, as well as provide them with some hands-on demonstration. Many libraries are using workshops as an opportunity to promote e-books and e-readers, encouraging readers to bring their own mobile devices. Given that many Americans are unaware that their local library lends e-books, this is a good strategy and one that is beneficial to both the library and the user.

Many libraries are now offering free workshops on e-books and e-readers to their users. This ensures that more users become aware of the e-book services available to them as well as how to access and download them onto their own mobile devices. Examples of libraries that have offered workshops on e-books and e-readers include Scott County Library in Kentucky, San Diego County Library, and the Lone Star College System. In addition to workshops on e-books and e-readers, libraries are providing workshops on mobile technology to various user groups. Purchase College Library in New York offers a variety of different workshops on mobile technology to their faculty and staff. Their workshops include "Mobile Technology: Apps, Apps, and More Apps" and "Mobile Technology: Buying Guide to the Newest Tablets, Gadgets, and Phones" (Purchase College Library 2014).

Library Displays

Library displays are a way to highlight mobile services and resources that are available at your library in a physical space. You can create a display to highlight a certain mobile service or resource, or incorporate elements that allow users to interact with the display using their mobile device. Scottsdale Public Library provides a good example of using library displays to promote a mobile resource. In an effort to market their mobile-optimized book recommendation Web app Gimme Engine, they created library displays using cardboard cutouts of their library staff. Each of the cutouts contained speech bubbles with statements promoting the service, such as "What does this busy mom on the go recommend you read today? Visit gimme.scottsdalelibrary.org to learn more" (Fifarek and Porter 2013). The library staff reported that the displays were hard to ignore and great conversation starters, which was what they hoped to achieve.

These are just a few examples of ways that you can market the mobile services and resources available at your library. Additional avenues of promotion may include the use of vendor-supplied materials such as posters, flyers, bookmarks, brochures, and images for your website. Being visible in your community is essential as well. If you are part of an academic institution, set up a table or booth at orientation or other events explaining some of the mobile services and resources available at your library. Regardless of which avenues you choose, make sure that you develop a plan and know what you want to achieve. Do not be afraid to take some risks, even if some of those efforts fail. This will allow you to gain an understanding of your audience as well as what efforts are not worth pursuing.

Key Points

Your library has invested in providing mobile services and resources, and you need to let your users know about them. Marketing gives you the opportunity to do that, and there are a wide variety of avenues to market your mobile services and resources to users.

- The library website is a good place to start marketing your mobile services since most of your users will be accessing information through it.
- The use of LibGuides is a way that your library can market e-books and provide your users with directions on how to access them from their mobile devices.
- Social media platforms like Facebook, Twitter, and Instagram are great ways that you can market services and resources to your users.

You and your library have now taken the steps to initiate, develop, and market your mobile services and resources. However, just as quickly as you have adopted mobile technology, it changes. The next chapter will focus on what the future of mobile technology might hold and what impact it will have on libraries.

References

American Library Association. 2013. "Social Networking." http://www.ala.org/news/state-ameri cas-libraries-report-2013/social-networking.

CUNY Academic Commons. 2014. "Best Practices in Social Media for Academic Libraries." http://commons.gc.cuny.edu/wiki/index.php/Best_Practices_in_Social_Media_for_ Academic_Libraries.

Dowd, N. 2013. "Social Media: Libraries Are Posting, but Is Anyone Listening?" *Library Journal*, May 7. http://lj.libraryjournal.com/2013/05/marketing/social-media-libraries-are-posting -but-is-anyone-listening/#_.

Ehmke, Cole, Joan Fulton, and Jayson Lusk. 2005. "Marketing's Four P's: First Steps for New Entrepreneurs." Purdue University Extension. https://www.extension.purdue.edu/extmedia/ EC/EC-730.pdf.

Fifarek, Aimee, and Ann Porter. 2013. "The Gimme Engine: A True Story of Innovation, Creativity, and Fun." In *Mobile Library Services: Best Practices*, edited by Charles Harmon and Michael Messina, 137–48. New York: Scarecrow Press.

Grant, F. 2013. "Expert Tips for Marketing Your Library." Association of European Research Libraries, June 3. http://www.libereurope.eu/blog/expert-tips-for-marketing-your-library.

Kotler, P. 2012. "Dr. Philip Kotler Answers Your Questions on Marketing." Kotler Marketing Group. http://www.kotlermarketing.com/phil_questions.shtml.

Mind Tools. 2014. "The Marketing Mix and 4 Ps: Understanding How to Position Your Market Offering." http://www.mindtools.com/pages/article/newSTR_94.htm.

Mui, C. 2011. "Five Dangerous Lessons to Learn from Steve Jobs." *Forbes*, October 17. http://www.forbes.com/sites/chunkamui/2011/10/17/five-dangerous-lessons-to-learn-from-steve-jobs/.

New Mexico State Library. 2014. "Library Marketing Plan Workbook." http://www.nmstatelibrary.org/docs/development/planning/Marketing_Plan_Workbook.pdf.

Pew Internet and American Life Project. 2012. "Libraries, Patrons, and E-books." June 22. http://libraries.pewinternet.org/2012/06/22/libraries-patrons-and-e-books/.

———. 2013. "Social Media Update 2013." December 30. http://www.pewinternet.org/2013/12/30/social-media-update-2013/.

Potter, Ned. 2013. "Marketing Libraries Is Like Marketing Mayonnaise." *Library Journal*, April 18. http://lj.libraryjournal.com/2013/04/opinion/advocates-corner/marketing-libraries-is-like-marketing-mayonnaise/#_.

Purchase College Library. 2014. "Faculty/Staff Workshops." http://purchase.libguides.com/workshops.

Rutgers University Libraries. 2012. "Multiyear Marketing Plan for the Rutgers University Libraries Spring 2013–Fall 2015." http://www.libraries.rutgers.edu/rul/staff/marketing/docs/marketing_plan_multi-year_2013-2015.pdf.

Webber-Bey, Deimosa, and Miriam Deutch. 2013. "Best Practices—Academic Libraries and Social Media." Brooklyn College Library. http://prezi.com/7hpjhhrq_rrr/best-practices-academic-libraries-social-media/#.

CHAPTER 11

Emerging Mobile Technology

IN THIS CHAPTER

▷ Emerging trends in mobile technology

▷ Interacting with emerging technologies, such as Google Glass and other wearable technologies, in libraries

▷ Understanding the impact that mobile technology has had, and will continue to have, on libraries

---

THE RAPID EXPANSION OF MOBILE TECHNOLOGY throughout society is, arguably, unlike any adoption of technology we have ever seen. Mobile technology has changed the way people consume and access information and has provided libraries with another service platform. It is becoming more prevalent, and many experts believe that access to information through a mobile device will soon outpace access through a personal computer. As innovation continues in the realm of mobile technology, institutions and organizations will face a wide array of opportunities and challenges. Libraries are no different. As the information behavior of users change, libraries need to adapt to those changes. If libraries and librarians are unable or unwilling to adapt to the changing technology landscape, they risk becoming less relevant to users as more of them turn to mobile devices and future mobile technology to meet their information needs. The future of mobile technology is bright, and libraries will have to adjust to meet the needs of users.

It is difficult to predict what the future of mobile technology holds, given the wide array of variables that factor into technology adoption. However, some mobile technologies are beginning to gain traction and offer tremendous potential. These include wearable technology, near field communication (NFC), and iBeacon, just to name a few. Some of these new technologies are features (NFC and iBeacon) that are being further integrated into mobile devices, while others are creating a new category of mobile devices (wearable technology). Additionally, these technologies will continue to shift the information behaviors of users and change how they interact with the world around them, even more than current mobile technology already has.

Wearable Technology

One emerging technology that is garnering attention is wearable technology. EDU-CAUSE Learning Initiative included wearable technology in their 7 Things You Should Know About series. The series provides concise information on emerging technologies and their implications for teaching and learning in higher education. Each part in the series focuses on a particular emerging technology. The publications address seven different questions that people need to be aware of. Those questions are:

- What is it?
- How does it work?
- Who's doing it?
- Why is it significant?
- What are the downsides?
- Where is it going?
- What are the implications for teaching and learning? (EDUCAUSE Learning Initiative 2013)

Before you can understand the implications and possibilities of a technology, you first need to know what it is. So, what is wearable technology? Wearable technology refers to devices that can be worn by users. It can take the form of an accessory such as jewelry or sunglasses or even physical items of clothing such as shoes or jackets. The benefit of wearable technology is that it can integrate tools, devices, power needs, and connectivity within a user's everyday life and movements (New Media Consortium 2014). This technology enables users to obtain a wealth of information regarding their surroundings.

How does wearable technology work? Most wearable technology focuses on a narrow range of functionality with a limited set of features. However, some examples of wearable technology are more complex, multifunction systems, such as Google Glass (EDUCAUSE Learning Initiative 2013). Some of the functions of wearable technology include providing the user with notifications received via text message and social media. The technology can also track fitness and health statistics such as steps taken during the day, calories burned, and heart rate. Some forms of wearable technology, like the Samsung Galaxy Gear smartwatch, also enable users to answer phone calls.

While wearable technology is still relatively new, some organizations are experimenting with its potential uses. For example, the School of Medicine at the University of

California, Irvine, has issued Google Glass to all of their medical students. They are the first school to implement the use of wearable technology into their four-year curriculum. Dr. Ralph V. Clayman, UC Irvine's dean of medicine, said,

> I believe digital technology will let us bring a more impactful and relevant clinical learning experience to our students. Enabling our students to become adept at a variety of digital technologies fits perfectly into the ongoing evolution of health care into a more personalized, participatory, home-based, and digitally driven endeavor. (Kerr 2014)

However, many of the uses of wearable technology remain experimental as institutions and organizations weigh the potential benefits as well as the drawbacks.

The significance of wearable technology is that it represents an evolution in people's relationship with computing and hints at a future of continuous connectivity. Wearable technology presents a list of potential benefits that includes monitoring the health of the users, which could enable timely medical intervention (EDUCAUSE Learning Initiative 2013). It can also provide video records of events. Additionally, wearable technology, in some forms, can incorporate an augmented reality overlay to real-life situations to enhance learning.

Regardless of the potential of wearable technology, there are some downsides. The most notable drawback is that the connectivity of wearable technologies, like Google Glass, raises questions of privacy, security, and information consent (EDUCAUSE Learning Initiative 2013). The main concern over privacy is that these devices can be hacked like any other device that sends and receives data. Other people can be recorded without their consent, and some of these devices, such as Google Glass, have been banned from certain establishments. In the classroom, there are concerns about cheating and unauthorized recording of lectures. Additional concerns are that the power needed to run these new devices will mean heavier batteries and increased heat, along with the perception that some of these devices are not fashionable (EDUCAUSE Learning Initiative 2013). Despite these drawbacks, many experts predict that wearable technology will soon enter the mainstream. In fact, wearable technology was a big part of the 2014 Mobile World Congress, and 2015 seems to be the year that wearable technology is poised to become more mainstream.

There are a variety of different ways that wearable technology could be going, depending on the aim of the device. EDUCAUSE Learning Initiative stated that wearable technology could incorporate haptic feedback, such as alerts to messages or upcoming appointments. The devices might also combine touch with location-based notification. Other devices might include biometrics for more effective security. An example is the Nymi wristband by Bionym. This wristband can unlock a laptop, smartphone, tablet, or bank account and confirms the identity of the user by their unique heartbeat. More and more companies are developing wearable technology. Samsung has released different wearable options like the Galaxy Gear and the Galaxy Gear Fit. Apple recently announced their smartwatch, Apple Watch. These developments show that technology companies like Apple, Google, and Samsung see wearable technology as a category with great growth potential.

There are a wide array of implications for teaching and learning in regard to wearable technology. This innovation has the potential to alter the landscape of educational computing by enabling the learner to engage in a variety of different functions. The EDUCAUSE Learning Initiative (2013) points out that wearable cameras could allow learners to engage as an observer, reporter, and participant. There is the potential for data gathering in biometrics and environmental conditions with less human interaction, which means less risk of contamination. Additionally, wearable technology devices could offer great assistance to people with visual, auditory, or physical disabilities (EDUCAUSE Learning Initiative 2013). These are far-reaching implications that have an effect not only on teaching and learning but on the broader society as well. This in turn means that libraries will need to be aware of and start evaluating the impact wearable technology could have on their organization.

Some libraries are starting to experiment with forms of wearable technology, most notably Google Glass. To this point, Google Glass is probably the most well-known wearable technology. It is a wearable computer with an optical head-mounted display that is activated by voice commands. The device resembles a pair of glasses, but it has only a single lens. It allows users to consume and engage with information about their surroundings, as well as collect data. Most of the efforts related to wearable technology in libraries center around Google Glass. Libraries are starting to explore the potential impact that Google Glass may have on the research and information behaviors of their users.

Google Glass is not yet widely available to the general public. For the initial release, Google had an Explorer Edition contest where users would post on Google+ or Twitter what they would do if they had Google Glass in fifty words or less. Several libraries participated as Google Glass "Explorers." One was Claremont Colleges Library. They began exploring the teaching, learning, and research potential of Google Glass in the spring of 2014. During that time, they invited poeple to submit proposals for how Google Glass might be used in teaching, learning, and research (Claremont Colleges Library 2014). They also held hands-on workshops so their users could interact with the technology.

North Carolina State University Libraries, Yale University Library, and Arapahoe Library District in Colorado have also experimented with Google Glass. North Carolina State University Libraries launched a pilot program in 2014 for selected faculty and graduate students who had an urgent research need for the technology. Requests were accepted from researchers working with augmented reality, innovative computer interfaces, and other possible uses (North Carolina State University Libraries 2014). Yale University Library took much of the same route as Claremont Colleges Library and North Carolina State University Libraries. They encouraged faculty and student groups to submit requests and proposals on the potential of Google Glass in enhancing classroom instruction and the research experience (Yale University Library 2014). The Arapahoe Library District enables users to interact with Google Glass at their "Goggle at Google Glass" events. Adults, teens, and children six years and older are able to interact with the technology at the events. The Arapahoe Library District feels that Google Glass is an important technology to have in libraries. Their website states that

> Google Glass represents the future of technology, and as a library we serve as an unbiased technological-literacy resource for patrons. We anticipate that Google Glass represents the first iteration of the "next big thing" in gadgets, and we want our patrons to have the opportunity to try it for themselves. (Arapahoe Library District 2014)

In addition to allowing users the opportunity to interact with the technology, there are a variety of other potential uses of Google Glass in libraries.

An article on the Open Education Database website by Ellyssa Kroski listed seven different ways that libraries can use Google Glass. Those ways are:

- Enhancing libraries tours by adding augmented reality overlays and imagery, along with audio and video files that explain the history of the building, library collections, and more
- Recording author talks and library events
- Enhancing "makerspaces" by giving builders additional technology that could provide them with helpful information like diagrams and instructional videos
- Recording hands-on video tutorials that give users the perspective of the creator's point of view
- Providing real-time optical character recognition (OCR) and text-to-speech translation for the visually impaired
- Providing real-time language translation of foreign texts
- Speaking to users in their own language with the capability of voice translations (Kroski 2013)

These are just a few examples of how Google Glass can be used in libraries. As the technology continues to evolve and become more mainstream, the potential uses in libraries will continue to expand.

Wearable technology provides a lot of potential for libraries. Addressing the question of how wearable technology might be relevant to academic and research libraries on the 2014 Library Edition Wiki of the Horizon Report, responses included:

- Wearable technology could facilitate energy efficient heating/cooling/lighting/security in library spaces by registering the number of people using parts of the building and adjusting energy accordingly.
- Language translations for communicating with patrons and also reading foreign-language books and websites; accessibility for sight- or hearing-impaired individuals—for example, books read aloud; new augmented reality apps will make these devices even more powerful by providing added layers of information over the real world viewed through devices such as Google Glass. These will be powerful tools for librarians as well as for patrons through lending programs or noncirculating use once the price point comes down. (New Media Consortium 2014)

Responses also included statements pertaining to privacy concerns, and that libraries and librarians need to be aware of these issues since some forms of wearable technology are essentially cameras. Librarians also need to be aware that many of these devices collect data and information about the surroundings of the user. Despite this, one responder noted that wearable technology is the direction that things are going in. As a result, librarians will need to be knowledgeable even if they are not on board with these devices. Regardless of where this technology goes, it offers another medium for libraries to reach users.

Near Field Communication

A feature that is becoming more prevalent in mobile devices, especially smartphones, is near field communication (NFC). NFC is a set of short-range wireless technologies, typically requiring a distance of four centimeters or less to initiate a connection. It allows users to share small bits of data between an NFC tag (similar to a QR code) and a device with an NFC chip or between two devices with NFC chips. The technology is currently available on different Android-powered devices such as the Samsung Galaxy S5. Apple has also added the features in the iPhone 6 and iPhone 6 Plus. Android-powered devices with NFC support three main modes of operation:

- Reader/writer mode, allowing the NFC device to read or write passive NFC tags and stickers.
- P2P mode, allowing the NFC device to exchange data with other NFC peers; this operation mode is used by Android Beam.
- Card emulation mode, allowing the NFC device itself to act as an NFC card. The emulated NFC card can then be accessed by an external NFC reader, such as an NFC point-of-sale terminal. (Android Developers 2014)

NFC offers a lot of opportunities for businesses as well as users. This technology enables users to pay for purchases using their mobile device, and users can share photos with their friends by touching the devices together. There have been various experiments with NFC at some higher education institutions. For example, Arizona State University partnered with HID Global to create a pilot use of NFC-enabled smartphones as mobile keys for building access (HID Global 2011).

In addition to the applications and implications for businesses, libraries have also considered the possible uses of NFC. Some libraries have used NFC tags to enable NFC-capable devices to access information. NFC tags are similar to QR codes, but they are able to hold more information. But while many mobile devices can download a QR code reader and scan a QR code, NFC tags require a device that has the technology already built in. This means that it is less accessible since a majority of mobile devices still are not equipped with NFC. However, there are still some practical applications of NFC for libraries.

One possible application is that mobile tagging allows for easier searching, locating, and circulation of books. Embedded information could contain bibliographic information, links to similar resources, or the due date of a book that is checked out (Swets 2014). The Hanno Library in Japan has used NFC in this capacity. Their library installed around one hundred NFC tags that direct users to Wikipedia articles on authors, pictures, and reviews (Nosowitz 2013). Additional uses of NFC tags include faster access to e-books and the replacement of traditional keys and library cards. These are just a few examples of how libraries can use NFC technology to interact with mobile users. As more mobile devices become equipped with NFC technology, libraries will look at new and innovative ways that this technology can be infused into library services.

iBeacon

Another mobile technology on the horizon is iBeacon. Trademarked by Apple, iBeacon extends location services in iOS. It is an indoor positioning system that enables iOS devices running iOS 7 and later, as well as other hardware, to send push notifications to other iOS devices in close proximity. Android devices are able to receive these notifications but are unable to send notifications via iBeacon. This technology enables retailers to send notifications, such as specials and coupons, to customers who are in close proximity to their establishments. The technology is still relatively new but is being tested in a few different capacities. Major League Baseball is implementing the technology, with twenty of the thirty Major League Baseball teams participating. Fans that use the MLB at the Ballpark app will be able to receive various notifications at different points in the stadium.

The notifications can help fans find their seats, receive discounts on merchandise and concessions, and queue up videos (Velazco 2013). The San Francisco Giants were the first team to implement the technology. Bill Schlough, their chief information officer, said that "it's kind of a no-brainer" when he was asked why they decided to implement it. He also stated that "mobile and digital experiences are paramount to our fan experience . . . and they have played a role in the fact that we've had 246 straight sellouts" (Gorman 2014). This technology has also been used by retailers like Macy's. There have not been any reported uses of iBeacon in libraries, but there is potential. This technology could enable libraries to send notifications to users about their accounts, events occurring in the library, and resources they might be interested in.

Wearable technology, NFC, and iBeacon are a few examples of mobile technology that are on the horizon. It is difficult to predict with complete certainty what the future of mobile technology holds and what impact it will have on libraries. However, one thing is for sure—libraries will have to adjust to meet the changing needs and expectations of users or run the risk of becoming irrelevant.

◎ Mobile Technology and the Future of Libraries

Libraries have traditionally been thought of as repositories of books, and most people still think of them in that way; however, the growth of electronic resources and the rapid expansion of mobile devices have shifted the focus of libraries. Libraries are no longer storage houses for volumes of books but institutions that provide users with access to information through a wide array of formats and mediums. It would have been difficult to foresee just how influential mobile technology would be just ten years ago. The information behaviors of users are changing more rapidly than ever before, and libraries must meet those needs. Mobile technology has provided users with a medium that allows them to be constantly connected to information when and where they want it. There is no doubt that technology is going to play a big role in the future of libraries.

TeachThought believes that the library of the future will contain more technology. In an article on their website titled "10 Ways the Library of the Future Will Be Different," they stated,

> Probably the most obvious direction libraries will trend involves more seamless integration of technologies at a faster, more sophisticated pace than even now. With so many exciting new gadgets and concepts such as ebook readers, tablet PCs, open source, and more, they have plenty of resources on hand to meet community demands. Books, sadly, do not hold the same collective appeal as the shiny and new gadgets, but enterprising librarians know they can still bring literature to the masses by utilizing its lust for technology. (TeachThought 2012)

In addition to technology becoming more prevalent in libraries, the roles and skills of librarians and library staff will continue to shift. With newer technology coming to libraries, library staff need to be able to assist users. In terms of mobile technology, this will encompass being aware of helpful mobile applications as well as the features and functionality of different types of mobile devices. In addition to seeking help accessing resources, users will also seek assistance with using their mobile devices. Library staff will need to evaluate services and resources to determine how they translate to the mobile landscape.

A trend that is starting to emerge in many libraries, and academic libraries in particular, is the creation of emerging technologies librarian positions to aid in the evaluation and assessment of new technologies, mobile included, and their implications and potential uses for libraries. Tara Radniecki (2013) points out that this relatively new position is being created as libraries attempt to leverage new technologies to update service models in reference, instruction, and access service departments to meet the needs of users in location, device choice, and information-seeking behavior. Examining job announcements on the American Library Association's website over several years, she found that the job duties related to emerging technologies librarian positions included the following:

- Trend spotting and implementation
- Website management
- Reference activities
- Information literacy and instruction
- Collaboration with internal and external groups
- Liaising with academic department
- Creating online instruction materials
- Technology assessment
- Social media/Web 2.0 outreach
- Technology training for both staff and patrons
- Electronic resource management
- IT systems
- Work toward tenure and promotion
- Digital initiatives
- Supervising
- Online reference services and collections
- Equipment and e-classroom management (Radniecki 2013)

The required skills for emerging technologies librarian positions included:

- Master's degree (general)
- MLIS or MLS
- Information literacy and instruction
- Reference activities
- Liaison/specific area knowledge
- E-science
- Supervisory
- Emerging/education technologies
- Digital initiatives
- Online instructional materials
- Technology training and documentation
- Website management
- Course management systems
- Programming and scripting languages
- Web 2.0/social networking tools
- Project management
- Communication and interpersonal
- Collaboration

- Ability to meet tenure/promotion requirements
- Mobile devices and app creation
- UX and accessibility
- Electronic resources management
- Systems/IT (Radniecki 2013)

Library roles are evolving, and so are the roles of librarians. Mobile technology has become an important focus for libraries, as has technology in general, and the skills required for librarians have shifted in the age of constant mobile connectivity. Mobile technology will continue to expand as new device categories are established and become mainstream. These new devices will further embed themselves with existing mobile devices and become a main, if not the main, point of information access for users. Libraries on the whole have done a good job adjusting to the mobile revolution, although there is still work to be done. Mobile technology will continue to shape the information landscape and offer immeasurable potential. Libraries and librarians must be prepared to evaluate and assess the changes that will be coming with mobile technology and determine how new and emerging technologies fit the overall mission of the library. The future is bright, and challenging. Regardless of where mobile technology goes, it will offer libraries another avenue to reach users.

⑥ Key Points

With the changing mobile landscape, new technologies are emerging that have potential implications for libraries.

- Libraries and higher education institutions are exploring the potential uses of wearable technology like Google Glass.
- Emerging technologies such as near field communication and iBeacon have some potential applications for libraries.
- Mobile technology has offered another outlet for libraries to reach users and has shifted the roles of library staff.
- As technology becomes more prevalent in libraries, emerging technologies librarian positions are being created to find librarians with the needed skills to evaluate and assess the potential applications of emerging technologies in libraries.

You have seen the value that mobile technology has for libraries and have taken the initiative to implement and develop mobile services to meet the needs of your users. As mobile technology continues to evolve, make sure that you maintain an awareness of emerging trends so that your library will be poised to meet the demands and expectations of your users.

⑥ References

Android Developers. 2014. "Near Field Communication." http://developer.android.com/guide/topics/connectivity/nfc/index.html.

Arapahoe Library District. 2014. "Goggle at Google Glass." http://arapahoelibraries.org/google glass.

Claremont Colleges Library. 2014. "Google Glass @ the Claremont Colleges Library." Claremont University Consortium, January 15. http://libraries.claremont.edu/glass.asp.

EDUCAUSE Learning Initiative. 2013. "7 Things You Should Know About . . . Wearable Technology." November. https://net.educause.edu/ir/library/pdf/ELI7102.pdf.

Gorman, M. 2014. "San Francisco Giants (and Most of MLB) Adopt Apple's iBeacon for an Enhanced Ballpark Experience." *Engadget*, March 28. http://www.engadget.com/2014/03/28/san-francisco-giants-mlb-ibeacon/.

HID Global. 2011. "HID Global Launches First University Pilot of NFC Smartphones Carrying Digital Keys for Access Control." September 14. http://www.hidglobal.com/press-releases/hid-global-launches-first-university-pilot-nfc-smartphones-carrying-digital-keys.

Kerr, D. 2014. "Google Glass Handed Out to Medical Students at UC Irvine." *CNET*, May 14. http://www.cnet.com/news/google-glass-handed-out-to-all-medical-students-at-uc-irvine/?ttag=fbwl.

Kroski, E. 2013. "7 Things Libraries Can Do with Google Glass." Open Education Database, April 18. http://oedb.org/ilibrarian/libraries/7-things-libraries-can-do-with-google-glass/.

New Media Consortium. 2014. "NMC Horizon Report > 2014 Library Edition Wiki." http://library.wiki.nmc.org/Wearable+Technology.

North Carolina State University Libraries. 2014. "NCSU Libraries Now Lending Google Glass for Research Projects." February 20. http://news.lib.ncsu.edu/2014/02/20/ncsu-libraries-now-lending-google-glass-for-research-projects/.

Nosowitz, D. 2013. "Use Your Smartphone at the Library, but Not to Read Books." *Popular Science*, July 8. http://www.popsci.com/gadgets/article/2013-07/use-your-smartphone-library-not-read-books.

Radniecki, T. 2013 "Study on Emerging Technologies Librarians: How a New Library Position and Its Competencies Are Evolving to Meet Technology and Information Needs of Libraries and Their Patrons." IFLA World Library and Information Congress, April 30. http://library.ifla.org/134/1/152-radniecki-en.pdf.

Swets. 2014. "QR Codes, NFC and Mobile Tagging for Libraries—a Big Flop?" February 13. http://www.swets.com/blog/qr-codes-nfc-and-mobile-tagging-for-libraries-a-big-flop#.U30n12JdXbO.

TeachThought. 2012. "10 Ways the Library of the Future Will Be Different." November 18. http://www.teachthought.com/trends/10-ways-the-library-of-the-future-will-be-different/.

Velazco, C. 2013. "MLB's iBeacon Experiment May Signal a Whole New Ball Game for Location Tracking." *TechCrunch*, September 29. http://techcrunch.com/2013/09/29/mlbs-ibeacon-experiment-may-signal-a-whole-new-ball-game-for-location-tracking/.

Yale University Library. 2014. "Google Glass Available for Faculty and Student Groups during Spring Semester." January 31. http://www.library.yale.edu/librarynews/2014/01/google_glass_available_for_fac.html.

Index

About the Author

Ben Rawlins is the assistant library director and digital services coordinator at the Ensor Learning Resource Center at Georgetown College in Georgetown, Kentucky. Ben has developed several mobile websites and applications for the iOS and Android operating systems. He has presented at several national conferences, including the LITA National Forum, ALA Midwinter, ALA Annual, and the Handheld Librarian Conference, on a variety of topics related to mobile services in libraries. He has coauthored articles that have been published in *Kentucky Libraries*, *Reference Librarian*, and *Mobile Library Services: Best Practices*. In addition to his master's in library and information science, Ben also holds an MA in history. He can be reached at brawlins4@gmail.com.